TRY ANOTHER WAY

TRAINING MANUAL

Marc W. Gold

RESEARCH PRESS
2612 North Mattis Avenue
Champaign, Illinois 61820

Copyright © 1980 by Marc W. Gold

5 4 3   86 87 88 89 90

Copies of this book may be ordered from the publisher at the address given
on the title page.

ISBN 0-87822-222-7

Cover design by Jack Davis

Composition by Omegatype Typography, Inc.

Library of Congress Catalog Card Number 80-52142

CONTENTS

ACKNOWLEDGMENTS

The following people contributed significantly to the development of this manual and to the technology it describes:

Penny Balicki

Lucille Brunet

Ann Buchholtz

Mike Callahan

Jeri Dolan-Arnold

Cath Dow-Royer

Ann Downs

Keith Edwards

Paulette Fernandez

Jude Fransen

Debbie Gibson

Ronna Gold

Lana Hilton

Marion Jay

Chris Johnson

John Johnson

Ann Kleiman

Ron Lecours

Rona Leitner

Lyndia Lewis

Barbara Lightsey

Maggie Marshall

Bill Montooth

Angela Novak

Linda Parrish

Bruce Ravelson

Fran Ravelson

Nansi Rhoads

Marianne Roche

Marcy Samuel

Sandy Schwartz-Malfar

Denis Stoddard

Mark Stricklett

Sharon Stricklett

Darryl Townsend

Joy Upchurch

Steve Zider

And, especially, to Charlie Galloway, who keeps me honest, and whose impact on this manual and this system is very deep and very appreciated.

USING THIS MANUAL

The *Try Another Way Training Manual* is used as a guide for Try Another Way Conferences, as a resource for those participating in Try Another Way staff development programs, and as a general source for those who wish to learn about the system. The manual alone is not intended to provide a complete picture of the Try Another Way System.

When special terms are first used in the manual, they will be set in italics. A brief definition will follow, and all italicized words will be listed in the Glossary as well.

The manual does contain some minor revisions of the system effective January, 1980. Four terms were dropped from the system:

1. Information — The term was replaced by the term "discrete steps."

2. Judgment — The term was replaced by the term "nondiscrete steps."

3. Procedure — Formerly, each Task Analysis had an abbreviated description of the interaction between content and process. The present Task Analysis form has a split page with content on one side and corresponding process on the other, making the procedure section obsolete.

4. Zero Reject — The term was dropped. The concept was made a part of the term "expectancy."

In addition, the meanings of Feedback, Content Influence, and Process Influence have changed; the new definitions are included in the Glossary.

SECTION 1

INTRODUCTION

TRY ANOTHER WAY: WHAT IS IT?

The Try Another Way System, developed by Dr. Marc Gold, is a training system which focuses its attention on those people who find it difficult to learn and who have been seen by society as different from most other people in society. The System provides a method for organizing and designing powerful training programs and uses many instructional procedures, some of which have been used in other systems.

Although the System presently includes strategies for teaching a wide variety of tasks to a wide variety of people, it is still not the final word in training. It complements other systems, rather than replaces them. In fact, it is only one of many approaches to providing efficient and effective services to people who find it difficult to learn. All of the other systems, techniques, and philosophies available should be thoroughly investigated by those who have a strong commitment to training.

THE PHILOSOPHY OF THE SYSTEM

The philosophical principles which shape the Try Another Way technology are as important as the techniques themselves. In fact, the action and thought which characterize the Try Another Way System have grown out of each other. Some basic principles of the system are as follows:

1. One can best serve handicapped persons by training them to do marketable tasks.
2. Persons labeled handicapped respond best to a learning situation based on respect of their human worth and capabilities.
3. Those labeled handicapped have the breadth and depth of capabilities to demonstrate competence, given training appropriate to their needs.
4. A lack of learning in any particular situation should first be interpreted as an inappropriate or insufficient use of teaching strategy, rather than an inability on the part of the learner.
5. Testing, at its present state of development, is at best limiting to the person labeled mentally retarded.
6. Labeling is both unfair and counterproductive.

These principles are reflected in the Try Another Way System's attitudes toward the learner-trainer relationship and toward testing and labeling.

The Balanced Relationship Between the Learner and Trainer

Teaching and learning depend on cooperation and respect. The Try Another Way System emphasizes establishing and maintaining a balanced relationship between learner and trainer based on mutual respect of personhood, abilities, rights, time commitment, and personal preferences and feelings. This kind of mutual respect leads to the recognition that both parties have a responsibility to adapt to the situation, eliminating "looking down" at learners. Learner and trainer find that they must adapt to each other not only in terms of the learning process, but also in terms of their human relationship. Quite simply, the relationship between a learner labeled handicapped and a trainer should be the same as any sound relationship between two persons working together toward learning a common task. A basis of respect and recognition allows each person the freedom to be himself or herself, adapting only for the sake of the relationship or the common goal.

To Pigeon-Hole or Not to Pigeon-Hole?

A balanced relationship implies a less categorical form of evaluating the learner than traditional testing. The Try Another Way System concentrates on deciding what a person needs to know for a certain task and then training her to do that task, rather than on fitting the person into a preconceived mold. Formal diagnosis and labeling can make it all too easy to fit the learner into a system and judge her by her label instead of by her individual capabilities. When this happens, the learner can get lost in a bureaucratic and linguistic shuffle.

Testing and labeling have practical limitations, too. For instance, the trainer usually has little interaction with the psychological examiner who diagnoses and evaluates the client. And because the examiner seldom sees the treatment or training activities, she bases her evaluation on a limited number of skills and tests. Both are denied important information about the learner by this system.

Tests alone are an inadequate method of establishing anyone's capabilities and needs. A test is a static device which measures a given item only at the time of testing—tests will neither definitively delimit one's learning abilities, nor say who a person really *is*. Thus, a training program based solely on formal testing and labeling may not expect enough from the learner, defeating the basic purpose of any training situation.

The most effective demonstration of a learner's ability and personality will naturally occur when he is actively engaged in learning. Because the trainer is constantly adjusting to changes in the learner's behavior, he is continually evaluating while teaching.

Such evaluation is derived from the individual learner, is suited to his needs, and is dynamic because the training situation is fluid. Much of the present system of diagnosis and evaluation, however, is tailored to the system, not the client. Just look at the number of existing organizations which are funded for the sole purpose of diagnosis and evaluation!

Even though testing and labeling may be necessary evils now, the trainer can counter their limiting effect by noting on the formal test report additional tasks beyond the test which the learner can perform. He can keep the test results as confidential as possible, even to the point of not letting other staff members see the results. And, most importantly, he can believe that this client's ability is open-ended, and use his own energy to prove it.

PEOPLE WHO FIND IT DIFFICULT TO LEARN

As already noted, the Try Another Way System is currently being used with a wide variety of people who find it difficult to learn. The original development of the system involved people labeled mentally retarded. As training went on, it became clear that the currently accepted definition of mental retardation was too limiting; learners were demonstrating much greater capabilities than they were "supposed" to have. An alternative definition of mental retardation became necessary.

Prevailing Definition of Mental Retardation

The current definition (since 1973) accepted by most governmental bodies and by most professionals is:

> Mental retardation refers to significantly subaverage general intellectual functioning existing concurrently with deficits in adaptive behavior, and manifested during the developmental period. (Grossman, Herbert. *Manual on Terminology and Classification in Mental Retardation:* American Association on Mental Deficiency, 1973; reconfirmed 1977.)

The following assumptions are implied in the AAMD definition:

1. Retardation is a general phenomenon.

2. Intelligence, as defined by tests, is permanent.

3. Defined intelligence is sufficiently general to describe all functioning and to imply potential.

4. Adaptive behavior includes both spontaneous adaptation and trained adaptation.

5. There is such a thing as the developmental period for all people.

6. It is useful to catalogue individuals according to their tested intelligence and tested adaptive level.

7. Mental retardation is most meaningfully conceptualized as a psychological phenomenon, existing within the individual, rather than the context in which he or she exists.

Alternative Definition of Mental Retardation

The following alternative definition is a much more optimistic perspective on mental retardation. It counters the currently accepted definition and represents the philosophy of the Try Another Way System.

> The mentally retarded person is characterized by the level of power needed in the training process required for him or her to learn, and not by limitations in what he or she can learn.
>
> The height of a retarded person's level of functioning is determined by the availability of training technology and the amount of resources society is willing to allocate and not by significant limitations in biological potential.

The following assumptions are implied in this alternative definition:

1. Mental retardation is not a general phenomenon. Every person labeled retarded has areas of normal capability, developed or undeveloped.

2. Intelligence, as defined by performance on tests, is a concept of little use.

3. No behavior clearly defines potential. Prediction describes what the person predicting knows about the environment in which the person labeled retarded will exist.

4. Adaptive behavior can be assumed for all persons.

5. Development is lifelong.

6. When testing and evaluation are the focus of attention, training is not likely to occur. When training is the focus of attention, evaluation must occur. So, train, don't test.

7. Mental retardation is most meaningfully conceptualized as a sociological phenomenon, existing within society, which can only be observed through the limited performance of some of the individuals in society.

The term "power" used in the alternative definition represents an important concept in the Try Another Way System. *Power* is the amount of intervention, assistance, or direction required by the trainer in order for the learner to reach criterion. The power for a specific task lies in the strategies and procedures the trainer uses in order for the learner to acquire the task. The more capable the learner, the less power needed.

Assists are a basic form of power. An *assist* is a trainer action—verbal, gestural, or physical—which conveys information to the learner about how to do the task. Assists for the more capable learner could include verbal directions, which have a small amount of power. For those who need a medium amount of power, an assist such as demonstration of the task could be used; and if it were likely that a large amount of power would be needed, the trainer could use a physical assist such as directly manipulating the learner's hands.

Other forms of power are motivation and reinforcement. *Motivation* describes any strategy, event, object, or activity that promotes the learner's desire to do the task. *Reinforcement*, a subcategory of motivation, is the arrangement of events that happen after a behavior to increase the likelihood that the behavior will be repeated under the same conditions. (Since the term reinforcement is used only for events which follow a behavior, it is separated from the broader term, motivation.)

Within the Try Another Way philosophy the expectation is that any individual, given prerequisites, powerful training procedures, and time, can learn any task in either a learning or social environment. No one is thought to be incapable of learning. This philosophy does not deny that all individuals have limits, some more than others, but it does recognize the impossibility of judging limits in the absence of powerful training.

How Society Defines People as Acceptable

Definitions, categories, and environments form society's perceptions about the acceptability of people who find it difficult to learn. They are subject to the same expectations and attitudes as all of us. Acceptance in society can be summarized by the *competence/deviance hypothesis:* the more competence an individual has, the more deviance will be tolerated in that person by others.

Putting that in perspective requires looking at the Try Another Way System's definitions of competence and deviance. *Competence* is a skill or an attribute that someone has, that not everyone has, and that is wanted and needed by someone else. Knowing how to use a punch press would be a competence. *Deviance* is anything about a person that attracts negative attention or causes discomfort in other people, such as making strange noises. Private deviance should be distinguished from public deviance. *Private deviance* is something that a person chooses to do privately which, if observed by others, would cause discomfort to the person doing the behavior, the people observing the behavior, or both. Picking one's nose would be an example. *Public elected deviance* is appearance or behavior that causes discomfort to others and that one can choose whether or not to do, such as swearing in public. And *public nonelected deviance* is appearance or behavior that is not under the present control of the individual to show or not and that can cause discomfort to persons observing, such as seizures or difficult speech. The absence of zero-order tasks is the most common form of public nonelected deviance. *Zero-order tasks* are those tasks or skills which attract negative attention if absent, such as dressing or bathing. Because society assumes everyone will do these tasks, their presence is usually unnoticed but their absence is conspicuous. As the term implies, when a person cannot perform a zero-order task, her value as perceived by others is diminished; on the other hand, if she can perform that task, her value is not enhanced. In other words, the ability to perform zero-order tasks leaves one at zero. To get a plus reading on society's "Who are you?" scale, a person must also have competence. For the trainer this means that persons labeled handicapped must be taught competencies as well as essential zero-order tasks.

How much a person's behavior is viewed as deviant depends in part on the environment. People act differently in different circumstances and are influenced by the opinions of those around them. If a learner never experiences any environment beyond her home and workshop or school, for example, she will never go beyond that basic level in her skills and will reflect only what others believe of her. This is known as the *chameleon phenomenon,* the fact that the behavior a person shows at any moment reflects who the person sees himself or herself to be at that moment. The phenomenon may also affect the trainer's *expectancy,* his belief as to whether or not the learner will be able to learn a task for which she has the entering behaviors and for which the trainer thinks he has sufficient power and teaching time available. The trainer must try to see the learner as she really can be, for what he sees as inadequacies in her may indeed be inadequacies—but of the environment, not of the learner.

TRY ANOTHER WAY TRAINING CONDITIONS

The Try Another Way System emphasizes correction which is not discouraging or harmful. For example, the word "no," however nicely expressed, is offensive. If it is used repeatedly, the learner will often stop trying. The expression "Try another way," on the other hand, can be said frequently without "turning off" the learner.

Try Another Way training more often focuses on providing information about the task, than on motivating or reinforcing the learner for doing the task. It is felt that too much emphasis on motivation and reinforcement tends to be distracting, to create an unbalanced relationship between learner and trainer, and to limit the ability of the learner to perform the task when the trainer is not present. The trainer does provide motivation and reinforcement where necessary, but with as little distraction from the task as possible.

This section has covered some of the philosophy and principles of the Try Another Way System. In the next part, Section 2, the structure of Task Analysis and key concepts and strategies are explained.

SECTION 2

KEY CONCEPTS AND STRATEGIES

ELEMENTS OF TASK ANALYSIS

Task Analysis is the instructional part of the Try Another Way System. A task is simply the activity which the learner is taught. The Task Analysis, discussed here, organizes that activity into teachable steps and strategies for instruction. The written Task Analysis is for the trainer's use, and while there is a general structure to follow (Figure 1), each Analysis is adapted to the specific task.

Task Analysis consists of all the activity which results in enough power for the learner to acquire the task. It should represent the most effective use of resources and time (*efficiency*). Task Analysis divides into *content*, the task and the steps into which the task is divided, and *process*, the way in which the task is taught.

CONTENT TASK ANALYSIS

Writing a Content Task Analysis requires choosing a method for the task and breaking it into teachable steps, while taking into account the learners' characteristics and the training goals.

Method

The term *method* refers to the way in which a task is to be performed. For example, there are several different methods of putting on a coat. One method is to start by inserting an arm into a sleeve and bringing the coat around to the other side. A different method starts by placing the coat on the table, inserting the arms into the armholes of the coat, and then bringing the arms up and dropping the coat over the head. For production-line tasks there are almost always job design alternatives, each one representing a different method.

For a particular task, the task analyst decides which available method is the best one. The availability of alternative methods depends on the creativity and experience of the task analyst or other available resource people. It is usually more difficult to identify alternatives with familiar rather than with unfamiliar tasks. For instance, when designing a Task Analysis for putting on a coat, the task analyst must take care not to restrict the alternatives to the method which she uses for putting on her own coat. With an unfamiliar task, such as the assembly of a milking machine pump, the task analyst may not have a preconceived method and, therefore, can explore alternatives without prejudice.

In writing a Content Task Analysis, a statement of the method used needs to be made only where it adds clarity to the Analysis. For example, a Content Task Analysis on the use of a knife and fork might include a statement that the European method will be used. Anyone knowing the European method will immediately know how the knife and fork are to be positioned and used. In most instances, however, the method is described through the steps of the Content Task Analysis and does not have to be specifically labeled.

Teachable Steps

The task analyst must break the task into *teachable steps*, which reflect decisions he makes about the necessary size and nature of each step of the task. In writing a Content Task Analysis the steps are numbered and described in detail, much as a set of instructions that one might get with an object that was purchased unassembled.

Figure 1 Try Another Way Task Analysis Structure

CONTENT (TASK)

Learner Action

Method of Doing Task
Teachable Steps or Components
Discrete and Nondiscrete Steps

Considerations
Entering Behavior
Composite Learner
Criterion I and Criterion II
Cycle Constancy

Formats

Single Pieces of Learning
Oddity
Paired Associates
Match-to-Sample
Simple Discrimination

Multiple Pieces of Learning
Backward Chaining
Forward Chaining
Total Task Presentation
Organized Exposure with Feedback

Combinations of Formats

Considerations
Task Characteristics
Criterion II
Control of Difficulty
Power and Efficiency
Length of Cycle
Trainer/Learner Time Use
Clustering Steps in Chaining Formats

PROCESS (TRAINING)

Trainer Action

Informing (how to do the task)
Trainer Provided/Task Provided
Before/During/After
Artificial/Natural
Verbal/Gestural-Modeling/Physical

Considerations
Timing and Power of Correction
Noninterference Strategy

Motivating (to want to do the task)
Trainer Provided/Task Provided
Before/During/After
Artificial/Natural
Verbal/Gestural-Modeling/Physical

Considerations
Strength, Frequency, and Duration of Motivators
Inconspicuous Feedback Strategy
Noninterference Strategy

TRAINER INTENT

Content Influence (knowledge)

Process Influence (affect)

The description of the steps, however, is only for the trainer's understanding of the steps of the task and is *not* intended for use as instructions to the learner. Nothing is mentioned in the Content Task Analysis about the trainer's behavior or the interaction between the trainer and the learner.

Steps can be discrete or nondiscrete, depending on the task. *Discrete steps* consist of content which is distinct or absolute. What is correct can be specified and all else is incorrect. Using a torque wrench to tighten bolts to 40 foot-pounds would be an example of a discrete step. *Nondiscrete steps* are those which have a range of correctness without definable boundaries, where a judgment is required. Using a box wrench to tighten bolts "pretty tight" would be a nondiscrete step. Nondiscrete steps are sometimes given a *guard-band*, a more narrow range of correctness than is needed. This is done so that after training, performance will remain well within the real boundaries of correctness. For example, if an object had to be threaded on a shaft to approximately ⅜ to 1¼ inches from the end, the learner might be taught to consistently thread the object between ½ and 1 inch from the end. This would assure that the real range of correctness would be less likely to be missed.

Other Content Considerations

The person doing the Content Task Analysis decides on methods and steps by taking into account the learners' present abilities. She must consider whether they have the entering behavior for the task. *Entering behavior* consists of the specific skills which are critical to learning the task but which are judged to be best taught prior to instruction on the task itself or which are already known by the learner. Thus, a learner who is going to learn how to shake hands will first need the entering behavior of a squeeze grasp. The person doing the analysis must also think about the characteristics of the learners who are going to be trained. A *composite learner* needs to be described for a presumed collection of learners, including age, physical and sensory characteristics, and amount of power generally required to reach criterion on the task.

To insure that content is really mastered, two environments are specified for achieving criterion. *Criterion I* (CI) is the predetermined point in training at which it is assumed that learning has taken place. It occurs in an environment created to maximize opportunity for learning the task. That environment may be (though it does not have to be) artificial. Examples of Criterion I environments include classrooms and counseling sessions. In a work environment, what is done after CI is called *production*. *Criterion II* (CII) is the repeated demonstration or performance of the behavior under the conditions where it is ultimately expected to occur. This is achieved in a real world environment. Examples include cooking at home or dealing with verbal abuse from strangers in the community.

The goal of CI and CII is to reach cycle constancy. A *cycle* is the total set of behaviors in a task. *Cycle constancy* is the reliable and consistent performance of the exact sequence or cycle of steps specified for that task in the Content Task Analysis.

PROCESS TASK ANALYSIS

Process means everything the trainer does to teach the content to the learner. The Process Task Analysis is a written description of the strategies the trainer will use. On the Task Analysis form (see p. 29), this description includes the areas of

Specific Informing Strategies, Suggested Hierarchy of Assists, Demonstration Information, General Strategies for Informing, and Strategies for Motivating.

Process Task Analysis is subdivided into format and trainer action. *Format* is the organization of the presentation of the content. *Trainer action* is what the trainer actually does to train a learner. It is subdivided into informing and motivating. *Informing* is performing actions intended to provide the learner with the necessary knowledge to perform the task; *motivating* is presenting objects and activities that promote desire on the part of the learner to do things.

Format

The steps of a task may be presented to a learner one at a time, several at a time, all at once, in the order that they naturally occur, or in some other order. Presentation will depend in part on whether the task is made up of single pieces of learning or multiple pieces of learning.

Single pieces of learning are task steps which can be viewed as standing alone or which the trainer feels are most efficiently taught alone. Selecting a house key from several keys is an example. If a single piece of learning is being taught, the task analyst may decide to use either the *oddity* format, in which the learner selects from a group of objects the one which does not belong, or the *paired associates* format, in which the learner acquires new steps by associating them with ones he already knows. A third format for single pieces of learning is *match-to-sample*, in which the learner is presented with one object and selects its match from a group of objects. *Simple discrimination* can also be used, in which two or more items are presented to the learner, who then chooses the item which is correct.

Most tasks involve *multiple pieces of learning,* groups of steps that are connected to each other in one way or another. Operating a washing machine is an example. If the steps are sequential, the training may use *chaining,* presenting the steps in a pre-determined order. *Backward chaining* can be done by presenting the last step or group of steps until the learner is performing them, then the next-to-the-last step or group of steps, and so on, until the task has been learned. *Forward chaining* begins with the presentation of the first step or group of steps in the chain until the learner is performing them, then the next step or group of steps, and so on, until the task has been learned. When chaining, *clustering of steps* can be used, starting with a group of steps and then adding several new steps at a time. For example, when the person has learned the last step, Step 19, then Steps 18, 17, and 16 can be taught together. *Total task presentation* may also be used for sequential tasks. The learner performs the entire task on each trial during training, and errors and assistance are reduced over trials until Criterion I is reached.

If the steps of a task are not sequential, the trainer may use *organized exposure with feedback.* This is often used to teach social interaction skills, such as getting along at a party. It begins with training in an artificial, controlled environment, and later moves through a series of approximations to the real life environment until inappropriate behavior is gone or appropriate behavior is reached at Criterion II.

More than one format may be used for any task, and formats may be combined. Deciding on a format or formats is subjective. What usually works best is to take each of the eight formats and think through the task using that format. Through the process of elimination an initial decision will be made. Considerations include the following:

1. What is the "natural" format, that is, the way the pieces are used in the Criterion II environment?

2. How much power will be needed in the Criterion I environment?

3. How long is the task in terms of number of steps and length of time to complete?

4. If the format used in the learning environment is different from the natural format (doing environment) how will the transition be made?

5. For the two chaining formats, how should the steps be clustered?

Trainer Action

Trainer action is the other subdivision of process and describes what the trainer actually does with the learner. It is broken down into informing and motivating.

Informing. Informing refers to trainer actions which are intended to provide the learner with the necessary knowledge to perform the task. The term is distinguished from motivating, which describes trainer actions dealing with getting the learner to want to do the task. In some cases informing can be motivational and motivating can be informational. The distinction between informing and motivating is something of a forced division; however, the distinction can be an important one when making training decisions.

Trainer actions for informing include a variety of options. The most open-ended is *exposure,* expecting the learner to figure out how to do a task without strategies to insure that learning occurs. Telling a learner to sharpen a drill bit until she knows how is an example. The trainer may also provide information related to the task or to the steps of the task, or uncover and take advantage of information provided by the task itself. Instructions, gestures, or comments on how to do the task made before, during, or after action by the learner are examples of trainer-provided information. These may include verbal or written instruction (before); direct manipulation of the learner's movements (during); and comments regarding the task provided about already completed performance (after). Color coding of parts, the natural characteristics of the task, and resulting changes in the environment which come from performing the task are examples of task-provided information. Finally, the information may be either artificial, for example, coloring one end of a shoelace, or natural, as in fitting two parts together.

When a trainer and learner start working on a task, the trainer knows at the beginning whether or not the learner already knows the task. If the learner does not know the task, he may need correction. *Correction* is the information that the trainer provides to the learner following an error; it sometimes is provided prior to an error being made if the trainer is convinced that the learner does not have the necessary information and feels that it would be more efficient. How much correction the learner needs depends on how much he knows about the task and the skills needed to perform it.

The dimensions of correction are time and power. At one end of the time dimension is "no delay," which is providing information before the error has occurred. At the other end of the time dimension is "self-correction," which is providing no correction (assuming that the learner has enough information to recognize the error and correct it himself). In the power dimension, "full power" means providing all of the information necessary for correctness. The opposite end is "no power," which is, again, self-correction.

The two ends of the time and power dimensions are easy to understand and to use. But the trainer must consider carefully how he will move along these dimensions. The two dimensions are independent in that the trainer can use a powerful assist with no delay, some delay, or considerable delay; but it is usually true that the trainer will proceed through each of the two dimensions, to self-correction and to correctness, at about the same rate. The following timing and power strategies are guidelines to provide assistance in moving along the dimensions.

Timing Strategies

1. When teaching a manual task to learners who require a great deal of power, the trainer should manually guide them through the entire task several times to provide a base of experience from which to respond to future corrections. This is a "no delay" trainer action. For more capable learners, demonstration of the task is a form of "no delay." This provides the learner with the opportunity to imitate or model the trainer.

2. Inform immediately after the learner makes an incorrect decision, but before she acts upon it. In some cases, especially with verbal responses, the decision cannot be observed until a response is made. In these cases the correction must be made following the error.

3. In the last stage of correction the learner is operating on internal information. She recognizes that an error is made and corrects it herself. Allow self-correction only when more might be gained from letting the learner complete the error than from catching it in progress, that is, when the mistake might be "obvious" to the learner.

Power Strategies

1. Each time an error which has been made previously is corrected, provide enough information to correct the error, but less than the last time.

2. Each time information is provided, the strength of the information should be reduced. Sometimes this can be done by providing less and less of the original assist. For instance, a physical assist may begin as manual guidance through the whole task, then be reduced to touching the learner's hands and arms when key movements are to happen, and later be further reduced to just reaching out but not touching at those times. In other cases, it is more sensible to provide new information each time an assist is made, but in smaller and smaller pieces which rely more and more on what the person has already learned. A group of verbal assists, for example, might begin with "Hold your right hand straight in front of you, palm down." Later assists might be "Which way does your palm go?" or "Hold it straight." Still later the trainer might use a short assist such as "Well?"

3. If you have an assist that works, don't use it over and over. Do not depend exclusively on the assists that work in the early stages of training for a particular error.

The first time a particular error occurs the trainer has three options within the timing and power strategies. One is to choose an assist that has a low level of power. If the assist has too little power, the learner will make another error on the same step and a more powerful assist will be needed. This could happen several times until an assist of sufficient power is used, resulting in a correct response by the learner. Some trainers feel that after three or four attempts at using low power assists, a strong "sure thing" assist should be used.

A second option when a particular error occurs for the first time is to use a powerful assist at once. The main disadvantage to this strategy is that it might take longer to diminish the assists than the third option.

The third option is to make the decision error by error. When the task analyst feels a particular step might be difficult and needs to be planned for, he can develop a *hierarchy of assists,* a listing of a sequence of less powerful to more powerful assists, for that step and write it into the Specific Informing Strategies section of the Task Analysis form. Or he can develop a hierarchy of assists to be used for most or all of the steps of the task, and write it into the Suggested Hierarchy of Assists section of the Task Analysis form. This is done when the task analyst feels that one hierarchy of assists will work for most or all of the steps of this particular task. In many instances both will be done.

One other informing strategy which should be mentioned is called the non-interference strategy. When the learner is attending to the task, find a way to inform him that does not require him to stop attending to the task. For example, the learner shouldn't have to look at the trainer to get correction on a visual discrimination task.

Motivating. Motivating, the other subdivision under trainer action, may be general or specific. It may come from the trainer, the task, or from somewhere else, and it may occur before, during, or after a behavior. Motivating may be artificially added to the situation or may exist as a natural part of the task or situation. Motivating strategies may be in the form of verbal interaction, gestures, or direct physical manipulation of the learner.

A distinction is made here between motivation and one of its subcategories, reinforcement. The term reinforcement is used here to mean the arrangement of something that happens following a behavior to increase the likelihood that the behavior will occur again under the same conditions. Since the term reinforcement is usually used exclusively for things that happen following a behavior, it is separated from the term motivation in this system, despite a considerable overlap in meaning between the two terms.

Most trainers rely almost exclusively on some kind of motivational system, usually a reinforcement system, as the primary source of power for training people. As such, it is important for trainers to recognize what can be bought with reinforcement and how much it costs. The following strategies describe the Try Another Way perspective on motivation. They require an understanding of the rules of behavior modification technology, so for those who do not have some background in this area, it would be helpful to do some reading. What is presented below is consistent with the principles of behavior modification, but is somewhat inconsistent with the way those principles are often applied.

Motivating Strategies

1. The best motivators are natural. Natural motivators are those which a trainer would expect to find where the behavior is expected to occur. For example, receiving a paycheck at the end of a pay period is a natural motivator for most working people. When natural motivators are used, there is no problem with transference of motivators from the learning environment to the doing environment. Natural motivators imply normal people. When an adult believes he is

being motivated in ways that are usually reserved for children, he often develops childlike behaviors.

2. The more artificial motivators that are used to achieve Criterion I performance, the more will have to be eliminated to reach Criterion II performance. Artificial motivators are those which are not expected to occur where the behavior will ultimately be performed. Being told how well one is working every few minutes is an example of artificial motivation, since it is not likely to happen in a normal work setting. Artificial motivators should always be temporary; they should be used only to establish a relationship or to get a behavior going. They should always lead to a natural system of motivation.

3. When the learner knows the trainer is attending, "no news is good news." With some motivational systems the trainer implies: "I'll let you know when you're right." With "no news is good news," the trainer implies: "I'll let you know when you're incorrect. When I'm not interrupting, you are doing fine."

   a. "No news is good news" is especially valuable when a person is learning a task she perceives to be interesting; the task provides the motivation, the trainer does not have to.

   b. The procedure is not especially good for teaching zero-order tasks. With these tasks, it is often necessary to use an artificial reinforcement system and then use fading to eliminate it. *Fading* is an instructional strategy in which the power of correction or reinforcement provided by the trainer is diminished as the performance of the learner becomes more accurate.

   c. A learner should not be allowed to work on tasks on which she is still making errors in the absence of a fully attentive trainer. If a learner has not reached Criterion I and the trainer must leave, the trainer should either take the learner or the task with him.

   d. If the trainer is using silence to provide feedback and a correction must be made, it should be done in a way that does not hurt. For example, the expression, "Try another way" can usually be used repeatedly without offending the learner.

4. When the trainer must interfere with inappropriate behavior that is believed to be for the purpose of gaining attention, she should interfere in a way that appears unintentional. This is known as inconspicuous feedback.

   a. Stop the inappropriate behavior in such a way that the learner does not perceive the intervention to be a result of his behavior.

   b. After "unintentionally" stopping the inappropriate behavior, provide some attention to the person who was indicating that he wanted it. The attention from the trainer, in this case, would not be perceived by the learner as being provided because of his behavior or demands, but because of the trainer's decision to do so.

   c. Once the learner's behavior is under control of the trainer, gradually reduce the level of attention to an appropriate level.

5. The trainer should find ways to motivate the learner that will not distract her from the task. For example, food should not be used as a motivator in speech therapy sessions for articulation problems.

For most situations it is not necessary to specify general motivation strategies in writing a Task Analysis. If the strategies described in this section are not sufficient, motivating strategies can be individualized for each learner. When a Task Analysis is written to increase, decrease, or maintain existing levels of a behavior the learner already knows, the Strategies for Motivating section of the Task Analysis might be the main section addressed.

RECOGNIZING TRAINER INTENT

One major element of the Try Another Way System which affects all trainer actions is trainer intent. *Trainer intent* refers to the effects that a trainer's values, experience, mood, etc., have on his interaction with the learner. Regardless of the decisions made under all of the categories discussed so far, the actual interaction between the trainer and learner will be significantly controlled by the intentions of the trainer. It is important, therefore, that the trainer attempt to recognize and control the effect of his intent on the person being trained. The two subdivisions of trainer intent are content influence and process influence.

Content Influence and Process Influence

Content influence occurs when the trainer consciously or unconsciously intends to focus on and provide the learner with information about the task. The following usually results from content influence:

1. The training interaction is less cluttered with motivational interchange.
2. The learner has increased opportunity to appreciate the task.
3. An environment is provided in which there is opportunity for the trainer and the learner to develop a balanced relationship—one in which there is respect and dignity in both directions.
4. The learner has less difficulty making the transition to the natural environment and to independence from the trainer.

Process influence occurs when the trainer intends to focus on and provide the learner with feelings regarding the task or about wanting to do the task. The following usually results from process influence:

1. The learner must understand and react to trainer action that has nothing directly to do with the task, for example, trainer feelings and trainer manipulation of the learner's feelings.
2. Control of the learner is emphasized rather than the exchange of information.
3. The training environment tends to be tiring for both the learner and the trainer because of the constant exchange of feelings.
4. The learner tends to be distracted from the information of the task.

These descriptions suggest a possible bias in favor of content influence over process influence. It is important, therefore, to point out the value of both. In those situations where, for whatever reasons, the learner is not motivated to learn the task, process influence is valuable and, in some cases, mandatory. However, when the trainer uses process influence to accomplish a goal, he must then ensure that the learner can maintain the behaviors without the process influence. This increases the total amount of time necessary for the learner to be trained. Many trainers have found that in spite of an initial inclination to intentionally use process influence, it is not necessary. They find that learners can learn complex tasks with an emphasis on content influence, and the training time is less than it would have been if process influence had been used.

Relationship Between Trainer Intent and Trainer Action

It is extremely important to understand the relationship between trainer intent, with its subdivisions of content influence and process influence, and trainer action, with its subdivisions of informing and motivating. Process influence can provide learner motivation, but can also intentionally or unintentionally affect trainer actions which are meant to be informing. And intentional or unintentional content influence can affect trainer actions which are supposed to be motivating. Informing and motivating are always a part of any interaction between a trainer and a learner. The person writing the Task Analysis systematically decides the relative proportions of each in the appropriate sections of the Task Analysis; but the trainer who uses the Task Analysis, regardless of what is written, will reflect her feelings and attitudes about the learner in her actions.

Trainer intent, then, is always part of a training session. It is important to be conscious of it and to be aware of its effect. It takes a great deal of awareness and experience to see and control how content influence can be superimposed on strategies for motivating, and how process influence can be superimposed (or systematically **not** superimposed) on strategies for informing. The key is to develop an increased awareness of feelings, facial expressions, inflections, and body language. This allows the trainer to separate, control, and take advantage of instructional strategies, the personalities involved, and the interaction between the two.

THE SEVEN-PHASE SEQUENCE FOR WRITING AND REVISING A COMPLETE TASK ANALYSIS

Once the trainer or whoever is writing the Task Analysis has established who is to be taught and what resources are needed, he then proceeds to do the seven phases described in Figure 2.

At this point the trainer decides on a method for doing the task, devises teachable steps, and writes them down in a Content Task Analysis. Then the trainer chooses the format or formats to be used, and writes that information down under Format. Next he decides how the learner is to be informed about the task and what forms of motivating, if any, will be used. The informing plan is usually listed under Specific Informing Strategies, but parts may be included under Demonstration Information, General Strategies for Informing, and Suggested Hierarchy of Assists. The motivating plan is written under Strategies for Motivating. Finally, the trainer composes the data collection form for measuring learner progress.

Then training begins. After all of the preplanning and analyzing, the trainer's job has just begun. In the moment-by-moment interaction between a trainer and a learner, trainer action should be viewed in terms of power and time, so that when an error is made, the trainer's reaction to the error will be "how long should I wait and

**Figure 2   The Seven-Phase Sequence for Writing and Revising
A Complete Task Analysis**

Phase 1. Decide on a method.

Phase 2. Write a Content Task Analysis (which automatically shows what method is to be used).

Phase 3. Write a Process Task Analysis.

      A. Write format.

      B. Write informing plan.

      C. Write motivating plan (only when necessary).

Phase 4. Begin training.

When a decision has been made that the Task Analysis needs revision (that more power is needed), do one of the following at a time. If Phase 5 doesn't work, go on to Phase 6, etc. There will, of course, be some exceptions to the order.

Phase 5. Redo the Process Task Analysis (format, informing plan, and motivating plan).

      Question A: Are there additional or alternative ways of informing or motivating that might work?

      Question B: Is there a different format that might work?

Phase 6. Redo the Content Task Analysis.

      Question: Are there parts of the task which are not being learned which could be subdivided into smaller, more teachable steps?

Phase 7. Redo the method.

      Question: Is there an altogether different way of doing the step or steps of the task which are not being learned?

---

how strong should the correction be?" At this point the trainer is guessing how much knowledge the learner has to react to each error. If the trainer thinks the learner has little or none, then the correction might use no delay and full power. If the trainer thinks the learner has a great deal of knowledge that can be used to correct the error, the trainer might allow self-correction to occur.

When a Task Analysis has been followed, people have been trained, and some of them have not learned the task, Phases 5, 6, and 7 provide the trainer with back-up systems. The order of Phases 5 through 7 was chosen for efficiency. Each phase requires less rework than the next. In some cases, however, the trainer will find it most logical or obvious to change the order. For example, with Phase 5, if visual discriminations were being taught using only the expression "Try another way," other verbal cues such as "Try another way, the flat part goes up" might be tried. For formats, if the original Task Analysis calls for the use of a total task format, changing to a backward or forward chaining format might facilitate learning. For Phase 6, if one step of the task is "Pick up the sock," this might be subdivided into "Point to the end of the sock that has the hole," "Insert thumb into hole," "Grasp sock by bringing forefinger down on outside of sock," and "Lift sock." For Phase 7, in making a bed, one can unfold the top sheet, then thrust it across the bed. An alternative method might involve placing systematically prefolded top sheets at the foot of the bed, at one corner, with the folds of the sheet being in a specific orientation so that the sheet unfolds into its proper position on the bed. When Phase 7 involves the selection of a new method, a new Content Task Analysis (Phase 2) must be written. It should also be noted that for any given task many methods are probably available, and for each method a wide variety of Content Task Analyses can be developed.

MEASURING PROGRESS

Measuring progress through some form of data collection should be a part of every training session. Every Task Analysis should have its own data sheet. The kind of sheet, and the kind(s) of data collected, depend on the nature of the task and the purposes for which the data are used.

To increase or decrease the rate of an existing behavior, the trainer should use some form of frequency count. A form indicating number of units, actions, or cycles per given period of time, or the amount of time required for a given number of them, would be appropriate. With some behaviors, like social interaction skills, the trainer might write down anecdotal information after each session.

When the Task Analysis deals with learning a new task in which the steps are sequenced, the data should reflect the accuracy (correct or incorrect) of the response for each step. One of the data collection forms used for this type of task consists of rows and columns (Figure 3). Each row represents one trial or one completed cycle of all the steps of the task. The columns represent the steps into which the task has been divided, that is, each column corresponds to one step in the Content Task Analysis. Some trainers prefer to use the rows for the steps and the columns for trials.

To record data, plus (+) and minus (−) signs can be used to describe learner performance on each step or blanks can be left for minuses when the trainer's hands are busy correcting the many errors early in training. Decisions regarding what will be accepted as a plus for any particular step of the task are made in advance of training. These decisions should be inherent in the step descriptions which constitute the Content Task Analysis. Analysis of data provides a clear picture of the learner's activities. The rows show how the learner is doing at any point on the entire task. The columns indicate the particular steps with which the learner is having difficulty and show progress for particular steps of the task. With learners who learn steps very slowly, even when a very detailed Content Task Analysis has been developed, more precise data are sometimes helpful. Instead of minuses for errors, the following symbols can provide the trainer with valuable information on how the learner is moving toward a plus: M (manipulation error); D (discrimination error); O (step out of order). Or the trainer can use numbers to record the level of assistance for each error: 1 (self-corrected); 2 (verbal); 3 (gestural); 4 (model); 5 (hands on, partially); 6 (hands on, total step).

The data collection form should also include the name of the individual being trained, additional spaces for the date of each session, and room for anecdotal information which might be of interest and which would not otherwise be shown on the data collection form. Time is also very useful information.

Figure 3 Data Collection Form for Task with Sequenced Steps

MG&A

Task Name Shaking Hands

Learner John Smith
Description Conventional Handshake
Trainer Jack R. Wheeler
Advisor John D. Johnson

Agency Osland Public Schools
Sheet 1 of 1
Total Training Time (minutes) 3
Criterion 3 consecutive trials without error

Comments

Trials	Date	Extends hand	Grasps	Squeezes	Up and down	Releases	Returns arm to relax	Errors	Trial Time
1	4/11	−	+	+	−	−	+	3	5 min
2		+	+	+	+	−	+	1	3 min
3		−	+	+	+	−	+	2	3 min
4		+	+	+	+	+	+	0	1 min
5		+	+	+	+	+	+	0	1 min
6		+	+	+	+	+	+	0	1 min
7									
8									
9									
0									
1									
2									
3									
4									
5									
6									
7									
8									
9									
0									

A data sheet different from the one just described, but very effective, is a form that was revised and used for 5 years at Project Skills, National Children's Center, Washington, D.C. (Figure 4). It is prenumbered and doubles as a graph that displays client errors over time.

Each row represents one step of a task. To record data, a slash mark is put through the number of each step completed correctly. No mark is put for steps not completed correctly, that is, those which required assists. At the end of the trial the number representing the total number of steps completed correctly is circled. Then a straight line is drawn connecting the circled numbers from all trials to produce a frequency graph.

Boxes at the top and bottom of each column leave room to record the date and the time taken for each trial. There are also spaces to record the name of the task taught and any unique task factors, the definition of criterion, the total number of trials completed before criterion was met, the total amount of time required before criterion was met, and the names of the trainer and learner.

VERIFYING ACHIEVEMENT

Criterion for any task taught should be repeated demonstration of the behavior under the circumstances where it is ultimately expected to occur. That means out there in the real world. It does no good to teach tasks to people who find it difficult to learn and see those tasks or behaviors performed successfully in the learning environment, and then not to verify that the person knows how and does, in fact, use those behaviors to improve his capabilities for dealing with the world. Because most of the training that goes on in human services is done in learning environments (false environments), it is usually seen as inconvenient, impossible, or idealistic, to think in terms of following the learner out into his environment to verify behavior. It is a major part of the Try Another Way philosophy that such verification is mandatory. Whatever resources it takes in terms of changes in trainer's time schedules, transportation problems, or communication problems with parents, other professionals, and the community, the cost-benefit ratio of such effort is extremely high. In fact, in the absence of such verification all of the resources utilized to teach the behavior in the first place are wasted.

When a trainer knows that such verification is a necessary part of training, the trainer will begin the entire process by describing clearly exactly how the behavior is to exist and be observed in the real world. This alone is likely to make training much more relevant and to steer trainers away from teaching tasks that have their only use in the learning environment. This verification process will also provide the trainer with valuable knowledge regarding what else to teach related directly to the behavior being considered and to other aspects of the learner's existence.

Figure 4 Prenumbered Acquisition Data Sheet

Data Sheet for: Telephone Dialing
Unique Task Factors: None
Criterion: 10 trials with 0 errors
Trials to Criterion: 19
Learner: Ellery Barker
Trainer: Annie Hughey
Total Training Time: 62 minutes

Scoring Code:
✓ = step done right
○ = total steps right per trial (column)
— = step unlearned

Steps

No.	Step
24	Good-bye
23	Identify self
22	Pause—listen
21	Phone number
20	Sample number
19	Phone number
18	Sample number
17	Phone number
16	Sample number
15	Phone number
14	Sample number
13	Phone number
12	Phone number
11	Sample number
10	Sample number
9	Remove finger
8	Move finger
7	Insert finger
6	H_1 transport finger
5	H_1 place pointer finger
4	Listen for tone
3	Place receiver to ear
2	Lift receiver
1	H_2 grasp receiver

Date: 8/2, 8/3

Time/Trial: 5/1, 5/2, 5/3, 5/4, 5/6, 5/7, 5/8, 4/9, 3/10, 3/11, 2/12, 2/13, 2/14, 2/15, 2/16, 2/17, 2/18, 2/19

Notes:

STEPS IN THE SYSTEM

Here is a summary of the steps to be taken in training using the Try Another Way System.

1. Decide what particular task is to be taught to one learner or a group of learners.

2. Establish what resources will be needed.

3. Proceed with the Seven-Phase Sequence for Writing and Revising a Complete Task Analysis.

4. Continue training after making adjustments according to interaction during training.

5. Collect data during training.

6. Use data to analyze progress in Criterion I.

7. Verify achievement in Criterion II.

This section has covered the instructional structure of the Try Another Way System. The following section, Section 3, presents the forms and checklist presently in use for writing Task Analyses using the Try Another Way System and for recording data.

SECTION 3

FORMS AND CHECKLIST FOR TASK ANALYSIS AND DATA COLLECTION

FORM FOR WRITING A TASK ANALYSIS*

INSTRUCTIONS:

1. *Fill in only those sections that are needed for the task being taught.* For many tasks the following sections are frequently not used: Tools, Equipment, Training Set-up, Additional Introductory Information, Suggested Hierarchy of Assists, Demonstration Information, General Strategies for Informing, Strategies for Motivating, and Other Information. Only include information that will be helpful to the trainer in those sections that are filled in.

A few specific examples:

   a. Strategies for Motivating — See Section 2. This section is seldom needed, unless it includes personal strategies for each learner.

   b. Composite Learner — Include only what will help the trainer know for whom the Task Analysis was written. A statement indicating small, medium, or full power must be made and interpreted subjectively to avoid a return to the use of conventional categories which are avoided in the Try Another Way System.

   c. Specific Informing Strategies — There does not have to be a specific informing strategy for every step of the Content Task Analysis, only where the task analyst thinks it is needed.

   d. Suggested Hierarchy of Assists — This section is useful only when the task analyst thinks a general set of assists will work for most steps of the task, and for most learners.

   e. Demonstration — A demonstration should be used **only** when the analyst thinks the learner will get something out of it.

2. *The form is to assist the trainer (or task analyst), not to force her to conform.* The trainer should feel free to include whatever she feels will work and to exclude whatever does not work. The more experienced task analyst will use the form and the checklist (p. 36) as a guide that will in no way inhibit her creativity.

The principal development of this form and the checklist was accomplished by Denis Stoddard, Mark Stricklett, and Steve Zider, with input from other MG&A staff.

**TASK
ANALYSIS**

ONLY FILL IN SECTIONS NEEDED FOR THIS TASK.
SEE CHECKLIST AND INSTRUCTIONS FOR USE.

TASK NAME

AUTHOR(S)

ADVISOR(S)

COMPOSITE LEARNER

ENTERING BEHAVIOR

TASK DESCRIPTION

LEARNER DATA

Learner No.	Trials to Criterion	Total Time in Training
1.	_____	_____
2.	_____	_____
3.	_____	_____
4.	_____	_____
5.	_____	_____

TASK NAME

PURPOSE

CRITERION

I —

II —

MATERIALS

TOOLS

EQUIPMENT

TRAINING SET-UP (Diagram)

TRAINING SET-UP (Narrative)

Location of Learner in Relation to Task

Position of Trainer in Relation to Learner

Description of Environmental Setting

ADDITIONAL INTRODUCTORY INFORMATION

CONTENT TASK ANALYSIS (Learner Action)	SPECIFIC INFORMING STRATEGIES (Trainer Action)

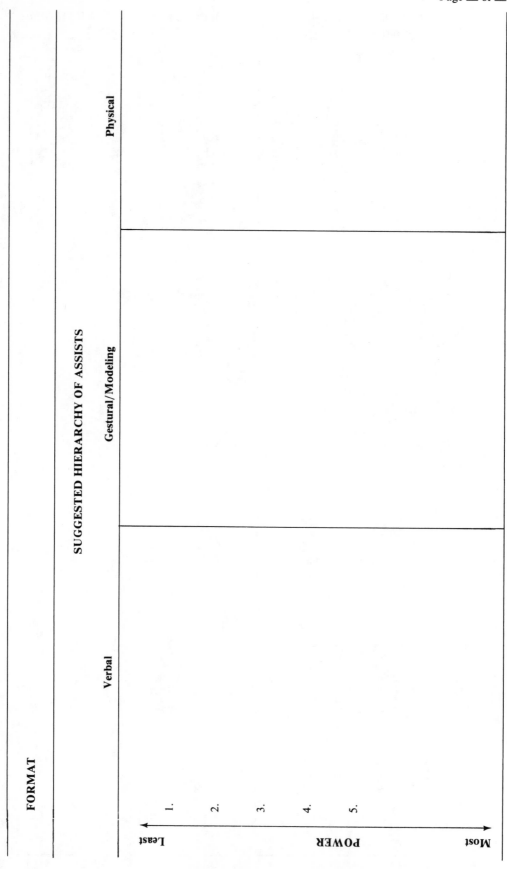

FORMAT

SUGGESTED HIERARCHY OF ASSISTS

Physical

Gestural/Modeling

Verbal

1.
2.
3.
4.
5.

Least
POWER
Most

DEMONSTRATION INFORMATION

GENERAL STRATEGIES FOR INFORMING

STRATEGIES FOR MOTIVATING

OTHER INFORMATION

CHECKLIST FOR WRITING A TASK ANALYSIS

INSTRUCTIONS:

Use this checklist to make sure the Task Analysis is complete. Read each question and circle yes or no, then revise the Task Analysis accordingly. If a section is not to be used, circle N/A to indicate this particular item is not appropriate or needed for the Task Analysis being written or evaluated. It is important to note that this checklist is for writing detailed task analyses which are to be shared with others or are developed by someone being trained in Try Another Way. Experienced task analysts will frequently create "shorthand" task analyses which give them the information they need to do a good job training someone, but which are not shareable with other trainers.

I. Introduction

   A. Task Name

      1. Is the task name, model, number, action, or use described?   Yes No N/A

   B. Author

      1. Is the author(s) name included?   Yes No N/A

      2. Is the author's name consistent with other times it has appeared (for instance, Bill, William, W. J., etc.)?   Yes No N/A

   C. Advisor

      1. Is the regional coordinator or person(s) assisting in the task development included?   Yes No N/A

      2. Is the regional coordinator's name consistent with other times it has appeared?   Yes No N/A

   D. Composite Learner

      1. Is the presumed collection of learners described in terms of age and physical and sensory characteristics which are related to learning the task?   Yes No N/A

      2. Does the power statement reflect the level of power generally required by the learner(s) for acquiring the steps of the task (for instance, small, medium, or full amount of power)?   Yes No N/A

      3. Have all entering behaviors been left out of this section?   Yes No N/A

   E. Entering Behavior

      1. If language is to be used, are words the learner(s) is expected to know listed?   Yes No N/A

      2. If there are any academic skills required in order to start learning the task, are they listed?   Yes No N/A

      3. If there are any motor skills necessary in order to start learning the task, are they listed?   Yes No N/A

      4. If there are any specific job skills necessary in order to start learning the task, are they listed?   Yes No N/A

   F. Task Description

      1. Is the name which appears in the "Task Name" included in the description?   Yes No N/A

2. Would a person unfamiliar with the task understand what it was after reading the description?   Yes No N/A

3. Are the statements in the form of behavioral objectives?   Yes No N/A

G. Learner Data (fill in only if the Task Analysis will be shared with other trainers)

  1. Are data from at least three learners included?   Yes No N/A

  2. Do the data on this cover sheet match the data from the working data sheets?   Yes No N/A

H. Purpose

  1. Is the reason(s) for learning this task described?   Yes No N/A

I. Criterion

  CI-1. Are numbers of trials and/or days to criterion stated?   Yes No N/A

  2. If some proportion of errors is acceptable under Criterion I conditions, are tolerated numbers of errors stated?   Yes No N/A

  CII-1. Is the ultimate environment(s) for the use of this skill described?   Yes No N/A

  2. Is the condition(s) for the use of the behavior described?   Yes No N/A

  3. Are numbers of trials and/or days to criterion stated?   Yes No N/A

J. Materials

  1. Are *all things* which are consumable listed?   Yes No N/A

  2. If this is a task that utilizes parts, are the parts listed and described using correct forms, consistent names, and identification numbers?   Yes No N/A

K. Tools

  1. Are *all things* which are not consumable listed?   Yes No N/A

  2. Are *all things* which are listed described with the appropriate name, model, and/or type number?   Yes No N/A

L. Equipment

  1. Are *all things* which are not consumable and non-portable listed?   Yes No N/A

  2. Are *all things* which are listed described with the appropriate name, model number, and/or type?   Yes No N/A

II. Training Set-up

A. Diagram

  1. Is the diagram neat and clear?   Yes No N/A
  2. Is the diagram drawn in black ink?   Yes No N/A
  3. Is the positioning of trainer, learner, tools, equipment, and materials indicated?   Yes No N/A

B. Narrative

1. Is it clear where the *learner* is located at the beginning of training and while the learner is learning the task in Criterion I?   Yes No N/A

2. Is it clear where the *trainer* is located at the beginning of training and while the learner is acquiring the task in Criterion I?   Yes No N/A

3. Is the environment where training occurs described to the extent that another trainer could create this training environment?   Yes No N/A

4. Is the additional descriptive information clear:

   a. Is the location of all materials/tools/equipment described?   Yes No N/A

   b. Are in-use and out-of-use positions for tools stated?   Yes No N/A

   c. If there are any special requirements for the task, are they listed (for example, ventilation, space, etc.)?   Yes No N/A

   d. If the quality control of the task is different from that of the criterion stated in CI, is this stated?   Yes No N/A

III. Content Task Analysis and Specific Informing Strategies

A. Content Task Analysis (Learner Action)

1. Are the statements clear and expressed in a few words?   Yes No N/A

2. Could a person read the Content Task Analysis and perform the steps if he had not seen the task performed?   Yes No N/A

3. Are all steps that the learner is to perform written down and measurable?   Yes No N/A

4. Is hand use specified, where necessary?   Yes No N/A

B. Specific Informing Strategies (Trainer Action)

1. Are there any steps of the task that are particularly difficult to teach and, if so, are the trainer's actions described? Note: it is *not necessary* that all steps in the Content Task Analysis have a corresponding step in the Specific Informing Strategies.   Yes No N/A

2. Are statements of trainer action directly across from corresponding steps of the Content Task Analysis?   Yes No N/A

All of the following categories are part of the
Process Task Analysis.

IV. Format

A. If a format for single pieces of learning is used:

1. Is the format stated in the correct terminology?   Yes No N/A

2. Are distractors (incorrect possible choices) clearly described and logical where oddity, simple discrimination, or match-to-sample are being used?   Yes No N/A

3. If needed, is there a progression of distractors from easy to hard?   Yes No N/A

B. If a format for multiple pieces of learning is used:

    1. Is the format stated in the correct terminology?   Yes No N/A

    2. Where chaining is used, are clusters specified and logical?   Yes No N/A

    3. Is there an explanation of what to do with the parts of the chain that are not yet learned or being taught?   Yes No N/A

    4. If organized exposure with feedback is used, are the environments clearly described and logically sequenced? Note: The description of these environments should be included under the section titled Description of Environmental Setting rather than the Format section.   Yes No N/A

C. If combinations of formats are used:

    1. Is it indicated where and how each format is used?   Yes No N/A

    2. If a sequence of several different formats is used, does the last format coincide with CII conditions?   Yes No N/A

V. Suggested Hierarchy of Assists

A. Are there at least three *general* assists in the verbal category?   Yes No N/A

B. Are there at least three *general* assists in the gestural/modeling category?   Yes No N/A

C. Are there at least three *general* assists in the physical category?   Yes No N/A

D. Does the second assist provide more information/power than the first? Does the third assist provide more power than the second, and so on?   Yes No N/A

E. Have all prompts that are specific to a particular step in the Content Task Analysis been *left out* of this section?   Yes No N/A

VI. Demonstration and Strategy

A. Demonstration Information

    1. If a demonstration of the task is to be used, are the following points included:

        a. Number of trials to be demonstrated before learner begins doing a task?   Yes No N/A

        b. Statement of how *trainer* begins a trial?   Yes No N/A

        c. Statement of how *learner* begins a trial?   Yes No N/A

    2. If one of the purposes of the demonstration is to lead the learner into some of the assists to be used, is it clear where and what the trainer will do to accomplish this during the demonstration (for example, verbal cues)?   Yes No N/A

B. General Strategies for Informing

    1. If there are any general informing strategies which are not covered in the Suggested Hierarchy of Assists, are these strategies stated?   Yes No N/A

2. Are these general informing strategies appropriate, given the amount of power to be used?　　　Yes No N/A

3. If language is employed as a general informing strategy, is the language the same from step to step, except for specific steps?　　　Yes No N/A

C. Strategies for Motivating

1. If there is a need for an organized artificial reinforcement system, is it spelled out clearly in detail?　　　Yes No N/A

2. If the basis for the Task Analysis is to increase, maintain, or decrease existing behaviors, is this specified here?　　　Yes No N/A

3. If an organized artificial reinforcement system is used, is the strategy for bringing the learner under control of the system clearly described?　　　Yes No N/A

4. If an organized reinforcement system is used, is there a clear set of procedures described to make the transition to a natural reinforcement system?　　　Yes No N/A

D. Other Information

1. If there is information relevant to the task that is not included elsewhere, is it included here?　　　Yes No N/A

E. Measurement of Progress

1. Is there a form for data collection?　　　Yes No N/A
2. Is the data form easy to use?　　　Yes No N/A
3. Does the type of data called for really explain what the learner did and provide the trainer with information for making decisions about Phases 5, 6, 7, Criterion I, and Criterion II?　　　Yes No N/A

**DATA COLLECTION FORM
FOR TASK WITH SEQUENCED STEPS**

INSTRUCTIONS

TASK NAME: Put the name of the task to be taught.

TOTAL TRAINING TIME: Figure the total amount of time required to reach criterion.

CRITERION: Criterion for acquisition training is defined in terms of a certain number of consecutive, correct, independently completed trials.

SCORING CODE: Use a plus (+) for correct steps and a minus (–) for incorrect steps.

ERRORS: At the end of the trial record the number of errors for that trial.

STEPS: Insert a word or phrase at the top of each column for each step of the Content Task Analysis.

DATE: Record the date the trial is performed.

TRIAL TIME: Record the time it takes to complete all steps of the trial.

Task Name

MG&A

Learner _____
Description _____
Trainer _____
Advisor _____

Agency _____
Sheet _____ **of** _____
Total Training Time (minutes) _____
Criterion _____

Comments

Trials	Errors	Trial Time

Date	Trials

Trials: 1 2 3 4 5 6 7 8 9 0 1 2 3 4 5 6 7 8 9 0

PRENUMBERED DATA SHEET

INSTRUCTIONS

DATA SHEET FOR: Put the name of the task to be taught.

UNIQUE TASK FACTORS: Describe any unusual characteristics of the task.

CRITERION: Criterion for acquisition training is defined in terms of a certain number of consecutive, correct, independently completed trials.

TRIALS TO CRITERION: Figure the total number of trials completed before criterion was met.

TOTAL TRAINING TIME: Figure the total amount of time required before criterion was met.

SCORING CODE: Put a slash mark (/) through the number of each step completed correctly. For steps not completed correctly, that is, that required assists, leave blank. At the end of the trial circle the number indicating the total number of steps completed correctly for that trial. Draw a straight line connecting the circled number of each of the trials to complete a frequency graph.

STEPS: Beginning with number one at the bottom of the page and moving upward, list a one- or two-word phrase that describes the step to be completed.

DATE: Record the date the trial is performed.

TIME/TRIAL: Record the time it takes to complete all steps of the trial.

Data Sheet for: _____

Unique Task Factors: _____   **Learner:** _____   **Trainer:** _____

Criterion: _____

Trials to Criterion: _____   **Total Training Time:** _____

Scoring Code:
/ = step done right
O = total steps right per trial (column)
— = step unlearned

Steps

Date:

A grid data-collection form. Each step row (numbered 24 down to 1) contains repeated column entries of the step number across multiple trial columns, with a blank box at the top of each column for recording dates/trials and a blank box at the bottom for Time/Trial.

Steps																					
24	24	24	24	24	24	24	24	24	24	24	24	24	24	24	24	24	24	24	24	24	24
23	23	23	23	23	23	23	23	23	23	23	23	23	23	23	23	23	23	23	23	23	23
22	22	22	22	22	22	22	22	22	22	22	22	22	22	22	22	22	22	22	22	22	22
21	21	21	21	21	21	21	21	21	21	21	21	21	21	21	21	21	21	21	21	21	21
20	20	20	20	20	20	20	20	20	20	20	20	20	20	20	20	20	20	20	20	20	20
19	19	19	19	19	19	19	19	19	19	19	19	19	19	19	19	19	19	19	19	19	19
18	18	18	18	18	18	18	18	18	18	18	18	18	18	18	18	18	18	18	18	18	18
17	17	17	17	17	17	17	17	17	17	17	17	17	17	17	17	17	17	17	17	17	17
16	16	16	16	16	16	16	16	16	16	16	16	16	16	16	16	16	16	16	16	16	16
15	15	15	15	15	15	15	15	15	15	15	15	15	15	15	15	15	15	15	15	15	15
14	14	14	14	14	14	14	14	14	14	14	14	14	14	14	14	14	14	14	14	14	14
13	13	13	13	13	13	13	13	13	13	13	13	13	13	13	13	13	13	13	13	13	13
12	12	12	12	12	12	12	12	12	12	12	12	12	12	12	12	12	12	12	12	12	12
11	11	11	11	11	11	11	11	11	11	11	11	11	11	11	11	11	11	11	11	11	11
10	10	10	10	10	10	10	10	10	10	10	10	10	10	10	10	10	10	10	10	10	10
9	9	9	9	9	9	9	9	9	9	9	9	9	9	9	9	9	9	9	9	9	9
8	8	8	8	8	8	8	8	8	8	8	8	8	8	8	8	8	8	8	8	8	8
7	7	7	7	7	7	7	7	7	7	7	7	7	7	7	7	7	7	7	7	7	7
6	6	6	6	6	6	6	6	6	6	6	6	6	6	6	6	6	6	6	6	6	6
5	5	5	5	5	5	5	5	5	5	5	5	5	5	5	5	5	5	5	5	5	5
4	4	4	4	4	4	4	4	4	4	4	4	4	4	4	4	4	4	4	4	4	4
3	3	3	3	3	3	3	3	3	3	3	3	3	3	3	3	3	3	3	3	3	3
2	2	2	2	2	2	2	2	2	2	2	2	2	2	2	2	2	2	2	2	2	2
1	1	1	1	1	1	1	1	1	1	1	1	1	1	1	1	1	1	1	1	1	1

Time/Trial

Notes:

SECTION 4

SAMPLE TASK ANALYSES

**TASK
ANALYSIS   SAMPLE**

**ONLY FILL IN SECTIONS NEEDED FOR THIS TASK.
SEE CHECKLIST AND INSTRUCTIONS FOR USE.**

TASK NAME
Refusing Someone When He/She Tries to Borrow or Take Money

AUTHOR(S)
Penny Balicki
Revised by Steve Zider

ADVISOR(S)
Mark Stricklett

COMPOSITE LEARNER
Adult individual(s) (above 18 years old) with hearing who require a small amount of power

ENTERING BEHAVIOR
Receptive Language: How are you; Do you have any money; May I borrow some money;
    I just want a dime; Let me see your money; Do you want to lend him or her money;
    You may not get it back.
Expressive Language: Fine; Not so good; Yes; No.

TASK DESCRIPTION
Two persons are faced with a situation where one person is attempting to borrow money from
the other. One person will be able to refuse lending money to the other person.

LEARNER DATA

Learner No.	Trials to Criterion	Total Time in Training
1.	_____	_____
2.	_____	_____
3.	_____	_____
4.	_____	_____
5.	_____	_____

TASK NAME
Refusing Someone When He/She Tries to Borrow or Take Money
PURPOSE
Assertiveness training to avoid being taken advantage of
CRITERION
I — Five consecutive trials without error or assistance
II — Three consecutive trials without error or assistance
    (See Description of Environmental Setting for description of environment.)
MATERIALS
Some amount of money, preferably the learner's own money
TOOLS
N/A (The sections where N/A is written are not applicable to this particular task.)
EQUIPMENT
N/A

TRAINING SET-UP (Diagram)
N/A

CONTENT TASK ANALYSIS (Learner Action)	SPECIFIC INFORMING STRATEGIES (Trainer Action)
1. "Fine" or "Not so good" 2. "Yes" or "no" 3. "No" 4. "No" 5. "No" 6. Seeks assistance if necessary.	Trainer 1 1. "Hello, how are you?" 2. "Do you have any money?" 3. "May I borrow some money?" 4. "I just want a dime." 5. "Let me see your money." 6. Trainer can continue to approach learner for money if she feels this would help.

TRAINING SET-UP (Narrative)
Location of Learner in Relation to Task
N/A

Position of Trainer in Relation to Learner
See Description of Environmental Setting.

Description of Environmental Setting
Criterion I : Environment 1 — A vacant corner of sheltered workshop with two trainers and one learner.

Environment 2 — In the cafeteria with two trainers and one learner.
Environment 3 — A random place where the learner is not expecting to be approached, with two trainers and one learner.

Criterion II: Environment 1 — During break time a co-worker will approach the learner in the cafeteria, and the trainer will be off to the side where the learner cannot see her.

Environment 2 — While shopping at the grocery store the learner will be approached by a co-worker or someone the learner does not know. The trainer will be observing from a position where the learner cannot see her and does not know she is there.

ADDITIONAL INTRODUCTORY INFORMATION
N/A

48   Sample Task Analyses

FORMAT
Organized Exposure with Feedback

SUGGESTED HIERARCHY OF ASSISTS

Verbal	Gestural/Modeling	Physical
1. "Try another way."	Gesture learner to begin.	Touch learner.
2. "Tell him/her."	Continue coaxing learner with repeated gestures.	Place hand on learner's back.
3. Verbalize learner action.	Mold mouth in position of word response that the learner is required to make.	Rub learner's back gently to relax him.
4.		
5.		

POWER

least → most

DEMONSTRATION INFORMATION
Trainer 2 will assume the learner's role. A demonstration will take place twice in Criterion I, Environment 1. The trainer will then motion to the learner to try to do what she has done. When proceeding to the other environments in Criterion I, a demonstration will not take place.

GENERAL STRATEGIES FOR INFORMING
If the learner hesitates, Trainer 2 will count to 10 before intervening with assists.

STRATEGIES FOR MOTIVATING
If at any point during the training the learner decides to lend the money, Trainer 1 will intervene after the learner's action with the following:
1. A stern look into the learner's eye.
2. "Do you want to lend him/her money?"
3. "You may not get it back."

OTHER INFORMATION
N/A

**ONLY FILL IN SECTIONS NEEDED FOR THIS TASK.
SEE CHECKLIST AND INSTRUCTIONS FOR USE.**

TASK NAME
Shaking Hands

AUTHOR(S)
Jack R. Wheeler
Revised by Steve Zider

ADVISOR(S)
John G. Johnson

COMPOSITE LEARNER
Functional use of right hand,* sight,* hearing; learners require a small amount of power

ENTERING BEHAVIOR
Squeeze grasp and understanding command words: Squeeze; Let go; Softer; Harder

TASK DESCRIPTION
The learner will be able to shake hands, using the conventional method, with another person as a spontaneous form of greeting.

LEARNER DATA

Learner No.	Trials to Criterion	Total Time in Training
1.		
2.		
3.		
4.		
5.		

*The sensory characteristics of sight and hearing have been included in this description for two reasons: (1) command words are being used, so hearing is required, and (2) the Content Task Analysis was done for individuals with sight who require a small amount of power. Statements regarding a composite learner's possession of sight and hearing can generally be assumed unless the learner is blind and/or deaf or, as in this case, the trainer has determined that this knowledge should be stated and is important.

Task Name	Refusing Someone When He/She Tries to Borrow or Take Money 0294	MG&A

Learner
Description
Trainer
Advisor

Agency
Sheet 7 of 7
Total Training Time (minutes) _____
Criterion

Trials	Date	Fine or Not so good	Yes or No	No	No	Seeks assistance												Errors	Trial Time	Comments
1																				
2																				
3																				
4																				
5																				
6																				
7																				
8																				
9																				
0																				
1																				
2																				
3																				
4																				
5																				
6																				
7																				
8																				
9																				
0																				

TRAINING SET-UP (Narrative)
Location of Learner in Relation to Task
N/A

Position of Trainer in Relation to Learner
The trainer will be standing directly in front of the learner, approximately 2' away.

Description of Environmental Setting
Training will occur in the staff lounge. Only the trainer and learner will be present after the demonstration.

ADDITIONAL INTRODUCTORY INFORMATION
N/A

TASK NAME
Shaking Hands
PURPOSE
To spontaneously shake hands as an acceptable social skill in greeting someone
CRITERION
I — Person responds with a handshake to a verbal greeting three consecutive times without error or assistance.
II — When introduced to three different people, who have never been introduced to this learner before, the learner responds by shaking the strangers' hands.
MATERIALS
N/A
TOOLS
N/A
EQUIPMENT
N/A

TRAINING SET-UP (Diagram)
N/A

FORMAT
Total Task

SUGGESTED HIERARCHY OF ASSISTS

Verbal	Gestural/Modeling	Physical
1. "Try again."	1. Gesture to begin or stop.	1. Touch learner's hand.
2. Use command word for learner to start or end action.	2. Place your hand or arm in correct position.	2. Guide learner's arm or hand to correct position.
3. Use command word to make action stronger or weaker.	3. Model step.	3. Manipulate learner's arm or hand through the step without completing the step.
4.		4. Manipulate learner's arm or hand through the step and complete the step.
5.		

least ——— POWER ——→ most

CONTENT TASK ANALYSIS (Learner Action)	SPECIFIC INFORMING STRATEGIES (Trainer Action)
1. Extend right hand to greeter. 2. Grasp greeter's right hand. 3. Squeeze greeter's hand. 4. Move grasped hand up and down. 5. Release grasp. 6. Return hand to relaxed position at side.	3. "Squeeze softer (harder)." 5. "Let go."

Task Name Shaking Hands   0472   MG&A

Learner	Agency
Description	Sheet _7_ of _7_
Trainer	Total Training Time (minutes) _____
Advisor	Criterion

Trials	Date	Extends hand	Grasps	Squeezes	Up and down	Releases	Returns arm to relax																			Errors	Trial Time	Comments
1																												
2																												
3																												
4																												
5																												
6																												
7																												
8																												
9																												
0																												
1																												
2																												
3																												
4																												
5																												
6																												
7																												
8																												
9																												
0																												

DEMONSTRATION INFORMATION
This task is demonstrated two times with another person before training begins. Following the demonstration the trainer motions to the learner to begin.

GENERAL STRATEGIES FOR INFORMING
N/A

STRATEGIES FOR MOTIVATING
N/A

OTHER INFORMATION
1. Arm is extended with elbow slightly bent.
2. Arm is approximately 6" above waist.
3. Approximately two up and down motions occur in complete shake.

TASK ANALYSIS   SAMPLE

ONLY FILL IN SECTIONS NEEDED FOR THIS TASK. SEE CHECKLIST AND INSTRUCTIONS FOR USE.

TASK NAME
Telephone Dialing

AUTHOR(S)
Annie Hughey
Revised by Steve Zider

ADVISOR(S)
Ila Reno

COMPOSITE LEARNER
Individual with use of one arm and pointer finger on the same arm who requires a full amount of power

ENTERING BEHAVIOR
Receptive Language: Hello.
Expressive Language: Hello; This is _(name)_ ; Good-bye.

TASK DESCRIPTION
Learner will dial her home telephone number, using a match-to-sample format, from her personal identification card number and will identify herself.

LEARNER DATA

Learner No.	Trials to Criterion	Total Time in Training
1.	_____	_____
2.	_____	_____
3.	_____	_____
4.	_____	_____
5.	_____	_____

TASK NAME
Telephone Dialing

PURPOSE
To enable persons to dial their own home phone number when necessary, using their identification card; to enhance communication and survival skills

CRITERION
I — Individuals will dial home phone number ten times with no assistance or errors.
II — Individuals will dial home phone number with use of identification card three times without error or assistance from a telephone located in the workshop.

MATERIALS
Data sheets, stop watch or timer, and sample cards with printed phone number. Example of sample card: 542-7841

TOOLS
N/A

EQUIPMENT
Dial telephone
Table
Two chairs

TRAINING SET-UP (Diagram)

Telephone and sample card are placed within comfortable reaching position.

TRAINING SET-UP (Narrative)
Location of Learner in Relation to Task
The learner will be seated at the table. The telephone will be placed on the table directly in front of the learner at midline.

Position of Trainer in Relation to Learner
The trainer will be seated to the right of the learner.

Description of Environmental Setting
Training will take place in an isolated classroom setting. Materials will be prepared and the training area will be set up prior to the learner entering the room.

ADDITIONAL INTRODUCTORY INFORMATION
The learner's phone number will be placed on the table, printed on a white 5" × 7" card. A black marker will be used to increase visual identification of numbers.

CONTENT TASK ANALYSIS (Learner Action)	SPECIFIC INFORMING STRATEGIES (Trainer Action)
1. With H_2* palmar-grasp handle of phone receiver.	1. If learner fails to start within 5 seconds, trainer will prompt, "Pick up the receiver." If learner doesn't initiate movement, trainer will model picking up receiver, replace, and then instruct learner, "Now you do it."
2. Lift receiver level to shoulder.	
3. Place the listening part of receiver to left ear.	3. If the learner has difficulty in identifying appropriate angle of phone, trainer models that the cord end of phone is placed at or near the chin and opposite end against the ear.
4. Pause for 2 seconds, listen for dial tone.	4. For initial trials, trainer will ask, "Do you hear the dial tone?" and then will check for dial tone and say, "Good."
5. With H_1* place pointer finger on the first number on sample card, left-hand side.	5. Sample card at right of learner. 542-7841 Points to first number of 7 digits.
6. Transport H_1 pointer finger to matching number printed on phone dial.	5. & 6. If learner points to incorrect number, trainer will instruct, "Point to the 5." For further errors, use Suggested Hierarchy of Assists.
7. Insert fingertip into the dial hole for specific number.	7. Numbers may appear on top or to the side or bottom of appropriate dial hole.
8. Move finger in counterclockwise motion, rotating dial to the right until it touches the dial stop.	8. In order to complete dialing, the finger must rotate until it touches dial stop. If learner releases before completing, trainer will physically assist and cue learner with "Until it stops," indicating to continue movement until reaching the dial stop.
9. Remove finger from hole at dial stop.	9. Allow dial plate to return to the original position.
(CONTINUED)	

*H_1 is the dominant hand; H_2 is the nondominant hand.

SPECIFIC INFORMING STRATEGIES (Trainer Action)

23. If the learner fails to say hello after the individual has answered the phone, the trainer will verbally prompt the learner to say "Hello."
24. If the learner attempts to replace the receiver without saying good-bye, the trainer will instruct the learner to say "Good-bye."

CONTENT TASK ANALYSIS (Learner Action)

23. Say "Hello! This is (learner's name) ." Identify self.

24. Complete conversation. Say "Good-bye."

SPECIFIC INFORMING STRATEGIES (Trainer Action)

22. Learner will be instructed to let phone ring 8–10 times before hanging up. If there is a busy signal, the trainer will instruct the learner to hang up the phone and redial in 5 minutes.

CONTENT TASK ANALYSIS (Learner Action)

10. With H_1 place pointer finger on the second number printed on the sample sheet.
11. Repeat Steps 6, 7, 8, 9.
12. With H_1 place pointer finger on the third number printed on the sample sheet.
13. Repeat Steps 6, 7, 8, 9.
14. With H_1 place pointer finger on the fourth number printed on the sample sheet.
15. Repeat Steps 6, 7, 8, 9.
16. With H_1 place pointer finger on the fifth number printed on the sample sheet.
17. Repeat Steps 6, 7, 8, 9.
18. With H_1 place pointer finger on the sixth number printed on the sample sheet.
19. Repeat Steps 6, 7, 8, 9.
20. With H_1 place pointer finger on the seventh number printed on the sample sheet.
21. Repeat Steps 6, 7, 8, 9.
22. Pause and listen for phone to ring.

(CONTINUED)

DEMONSTRATION INFORMATION

The trainer will begin the session by instructing the learner to "watch." The trainer will demonstrate the entire task (see content steps), verbally repeating each number as dialed. The trainer will call the learner's home phone number, identifying himself, and let the person answering know that the learner will call in a few minutes for the training exercise. Upon completion, the trainer will instruct the learner to dial her phone number with the verbal cue "Make your phone call."

GENERAL STRATEGIES FOR INFORMING

N/A

STRATEGIES FOR MOTIVATING

N/A

OTHER INFORMATION

This task analysis is designed to instruct the learner to dial her phone number, which she will carry in her possession on an identification card. The sample card (5″ × 7″) will be reduced in size over trials until the learner can dial the phone number using her identification card.

Arrangements will be made with family members who are at home to expect the calls. They will be instructed not to hang up until the learner has greeted them appropriately, has identified herself, and has said good-bye at the end of the conversation.

If a learner is having extreme difficulty with discrimination of the numbers, the trainer can cover all numbers but the number to be dialed on the phone, the card, or both, and move the cover after each number.

FORMAT

Match-to-Sample using a Total Task Presentation

SUGGESTED HIERARCHY OF ASSISTS

Verbal	Gestural/Modeling	Physical
1. "Try another way."	Point in the general direction of sample card/phone.	Gently touch the learner.
2. "Try another place."	Point within 3″ of the sample card/phone/faceplate.	Guide the learner partially through the step.
3. "Try another number."	Point within 1″ of the sample card, correct number/phone.	
4. Specific verbal cue. Example: "Point to 1." (Point to specific number.)	Point directly to the correct number.	Guide the learner through the step by grasping the learner's hand and manipulating it through the step.
5.	Model the step.	

POWER: least → most

TASK ANALYSIS **SAMPLE**

ONLY FILL IN SECTIONS NEEDED FOR THIS TASK.
SEE CHECKLIST AND INSTRUCTIONS FOR USE.

TASK NAME
Stringing an Ektalon Metal Racquetball Racquet

AUTHOR(S)
Donna Dowell, Jim Hamilton, Bob Pray

ADVISOR(S)
Christine Johnson

COMPOSITE LEARNER
Adult individual with functional use of all limbs and hearing who requires a moderate amount of power

ENTERING BEHAVIOR

Task Name	*T.A. No.*	*Job Station No.*	*Language Required*
Mounting the String Clamps	1	I	Receptive: Together; Closer; Put it down Expressive: None
Locating Center Holes on Racquet Using the Centering Jig	2	II	Receptive: Match the lines; Press down; Tighter Expressive: None
Placing the Racquet in the Stringing Machine	3	II	Receptive: Match the lines Expressive: None
Positioning the Racquet	4	II	Receptive: None Expressive: None
Preparing the String	5	III	Receptive: Hold string tighter Expressive: None
Stringing the Mainstrings	6	IV	Receptive: Next to line Expressive: None
Tensioning the Mainstrings	7	IV	Receptive: None Expressive: None
Knot Tying	8	V	Receptive: Hold loop straight; Hold pliers tighter Expressive: None
Waxing and Stringing Cross Strings	9	VI	Receptive: Start here; Too much; Over; Under; Insert here; Weave Expressive: Over; Under

Scoring Code:
/ = step done right
◯ = total steps right per trial (column)
_ = step unlearned

Data Sheet for: Telephone Dialing
Unique Task Factors: ______ **Learner:** ______ **Trainer:** ______
Criterion: ______
Trials to Criterion: ______ **Total Training Time:** ______

Steps																								
Date:																								
24	Good-bye	24	24	24	24	24	24	24	24	24	24	24	24	24	24	24	24	24	24	24	24	24	24	24
23	Identify self	23	23	23	23	23	23	23	23	23	23	23	23	23	23	23	23	23	23	23	23	23	23	23
22	Pause—listen	22	22	22	22	22	22	22	22	22	22	22	22	22	22	22	22	22	22	22	22	22	22	22
21	Phone number	21	21	21	21	21	21	21	21	21	21	21	21	21	21	21	21	21	21	21	21	21	21	21
20	Sample number	20	20	20	20	20	20	20	20	20	20	20	20	20	20	20	20	20	20	20	20	20	20	20
19	Phone number	19	19	19	19	19	19	19	19	19	19	19	19	19	19	19	19	19	19	19	19	19	19	19
18	Sample number	18	18	18	18	18	18	18	18	18	18	18	18	18	18	18	18	18	18	18	18	18	18	18
17	Phone number	17	17	17	17	17	17	17	17	17	17	17	17	17	17	17	17	17	17	17	17	17	17	17
16	Sample number	16	16	16	16	16	16	16	16	16	16	16	16	16	16	16	16	16	16	16	16	16	16	16
15	Phone number	15	15	15	15	15	15	15	15	15	15	15	15	15	15	15	15	15	15	15	15	15	15	15
14	Sample number	14	14	14	14	14	14	14	14	14	14	14	14	14	14	14	14	14	14	14	14	14	14	14
13	Phone number	13	13	13	13	13	13	13	13	13	13	13	13	13	13	13	13	13	13	13	13	13	13	13
12	Sample number	12	12	12	12	12	12	12	12	12	12	12	12	12	12	12	12	12	12	12	12	12	12	12
11	Phone number	11	11	11	11	11	11	11	11	11	11	11	11	11	11	11	11	11	11	11	11	11	11	11
10	Sample number	10	10	10	10	10	10	10	10	10	10	10	10	10	10	10	10	10	10	10	10	10	10	10
9	Remove finger	9	9	9	9	9	9	9	9	9	9	9	9	9	9	9	9	9	9	9	9	9	9	9
8	Move finger	8	8	8	8	8	8	8	8	8	8	8	8	8	8	8	8	8	8	8	8	8	8	8
7	Insert finger	7	7	7	7	7	7	7	7	7	7	7	7	7	7	7	7	7	7	7	7	7	7	7
6	H_1 transport finger	6	6	6	6	6	6	6	6	6	6	6	6	6	6	6	6	6	6	6	6	6	6	6
5	H_1 place pointer finger	5	5	5	5	5	5	5	5	5	5	5	5	5	5	5	5	5	5	5	5	5	5	5
4	Listen for tone	4	4	4	4	4	4	4	4	4	4	4	4	4	4	4	4	4	4	4	4	4	4	4
3	Place receiver to ear	3	3	3	3	3	3	3	3	3	3	3	3	3	3	3	3	3	3	3	3	3	3	3
2	Lift receiver	2	2	2	2	2	2	2	2	2	2	2	2	2	2	2	2	2	2	2	2	2	2	2
1	H_2 grasp receiver	1	1	1	1	1	1	1	1	1	1	1	1	1	1	1	1	1	1	1	1	1	1	1
	Time/Trial																							

Notes:

TASK DESCRIPTION

This task consists of nine separate Task Analyses. The learner will perform over 500 steps that will result in a completely strung and pressure-tested racquet. Learners will cut, prepare, clamp, string, tension, knot, and weave the racquet. Six different job stations are used in the assembly process.

LEARNER DATA

Learner No.	Trials to Criterion	Total Time in Training
1.	_____	_____
2.	_____	_____
3.	_____	_____
4.	_____	_____
5.	_____	_____

TASK NAME

Mounting the String Clamps — T.A. 1 (Job Station I)

PURPOSE

Same as above

CRITERION

I — Three correct consecutive trials without error or assistance
II — Three correct consecutive trials without error or assistance at the work station located in the sheltered workshop

MATERIALS

N/A

TOOLS

Two string clamps; two glide bars; two tool tray castings

EQUIPMENT

One Ektalon Model D racquet-stringing machine

TRAINING SET-UP (Diagram)

N/A

TRAINING SET-UP (Narrative)

Location of Learner in Relation to Task
The learner will be standing directly in front of the stringing machine.

Position of Trainer in Relation to Learner
The trainer will be standing to the left of the learner.

Description of Environmental Setting
Training during Criterion I will take place in an isolated room where only the trainer and learner are present. The lighting must be adequate for fine visual work.

ADDITIONAL INTRODUCTORY INFORMATION

N/A

CONTENT TASK ANALYSIS (Learner Action)	SPECIFIC INFORMING STRATEGIES (Trainer Action)
1. Grasp clamp H_1 so that jaws are between index finger and thumb.	
2. Position lever on side of thumb.	
3. Grasp lever with H_2.	
4. Lift lever with H_2.	
5. Pinch jaws with H_1 until foot of clamp is open.	
6. Release H_2.	
7. Pick up glide bar with H_2.	
8. Position tapered ends of bar pointing toward learner.	8. "Turn"
9. Position grooved foot of string clamp on glide bar with H_1.	
10. Slide string clamp with H_1 between thumb and index finger of H_2.	
11. Grasp with H_2 approximately 1" from H_2 end of bar.	
12. Pincer grasp string clamp lever with H_1, index finger under curved area of lever.	
13. Pull and lift lever to insert bottom point of lever into place.	
14. Hold bar, end piece, on H_1 end with H_1 thumb positioned in line with bar and index finger aligned under thumb, fingers grasping lower edge.	
15. Rotate string clamp 90° so that string clamp lever points toward ceiling.	
16. Lower assembly until string clamp rests on frame table.	16. "Put it down."
17. Release H_2.	
18. Grasp H_2 side of glide bar in same manner as H_1.	
19. Align glide bar glides with frame table rail slots.	19. "Together, closer."
20. Insert glides into slots until end pieces are entirely on rail.	
21. Grasp racquet handle with H_2.	
22. Rotate racquet 180° (releasing brake lever if frame table does not freely rotate).	
23. Repeat Steps 18–22.	

DEMONSTRATION INFORMATION
The trainer will demonstrate the entire task twice. The trainer will then motion to the learner to begin. After this initial procedure, the string clamps will only be mounted if they are not already positioned on the machine.

GENERAL STRATEGIES FOR INFORMING
N/A

STRATEGIES FOR MOTIVATING
N/A

OTHER INFORMATION
Step 4: The lever has two positions. The first position opens the teeth and the second position opens the foot. When mounting, the lever should be in the second position. When clamping, the lever should be in the first position.

FORMAT
Forward Chaining

SUGGESTED HIERARCHY OF ASSISTS*

Verbal	Gestural/Modeling	Physical
1. "Try another way."	Gesture learner to begin.	Touch the learner's elbow.
2. Use command word for learner to start or end action.	Point to the part or hand.	Guide the learner's arm or hand to the action required.
3. Use command word to make action stronger or weaker.	Model the step partially.	Begin to manipulate the learner's arm or hand to the correct action.
4. Use specific language to further guide learner action.	Model the entire step.	Directly manipulate the learner's arm or hand through the step but do not complete the entire step.
5.		Directly manipulate the learner's arm or hand through the entire step.

least — POWER — most

*This general hierarchy can be used with all Task Analyses included in this package. There are several specific assists for particular analyses. For those specific assists please refer to the Trainer Action sections of those particular analyses.

TASK NAME
Locating Center Holes on Racquet Using the Centering Jig — T.A. 2 (Job Station II)
PURPOSE
Same as above
CRITERION
I — Three correct consecutive trials without error or assistance
II — Three correct consecutive trials without error or assistance at the work station located in the sheltered workshop
MATERIALS
One grease pencil; one unstrung racquet
TOOLS
N/A
EQUIPMENT
One centering jig

TRAINING SET-UP (Diagram)
N/A

TRAINING SET-UP (Narrative)
Location of Learner in Relation to Task
The learner will be seated at a work table with the centering jig directly in front of him.
Position of Trainer in Relation to Learner
The trainer will be standing directly in back of the learner.
Description of Environmental Setting
Training will take place in an isolated room with a work table, one chair, and adequate lighting.

ADDITIONAL INTRODUCTORY INFORMATION
N/A

Task Name	Mounting the String Clamps — T.A. 1 (Job Station I)	MG&A

Learner	Agency
Description	Sheet 6 of 48
Trainer	Total Training Time (minutes) _____
Advisor	Criterion

Trials	Date	Grasp H₁	Position lever	Grasp H₂	Lift H₁	Pinch H₁	Release H₁	Pick up H₂	Position	Position	Slide	Grasp H₂	Pincer grasp H₁	Pull/Lift	Hold	Rotate	Lower	Release H₂	Grasp H₂	Align	Insert	Grasp H₂	Rotate	Repeat 18–22										Errors	Trial Time	Comments
1																																				
2																																				
3																																				
4																																				
5																																				
6																																				
7																																				
8																																				
9																																				
0																																				
1																																				
2																																				
3																																				
4																																				
5																																				
6																																				
7																																				
8																																				
9																																				
0																																				

CONTENT TASK ANALYSIS (Learner Action)	SPECIFIC INFORMING STRATEGIES (Trainer Action)
1. Place unstrung racquet on jig with H_1 so that board is raised horizontally and is encompassed by unstrung racquet.	
2. Hold jig steady by pushing downward on jig with H_2 fingertips.	2. "Press down."
3. Position H_2 fingertips in center of unstrung racquet.	3. Stand with throat clamp in front of left hand and tip clamp in front of right hand.
4. Slide racquet away from learner until throat piece edges of racquet rest firmly against corners of raised horizontal bar closest to learner.	
5. Release H_2.	
6. Place fingertips of H_2 over edge of raised horizontal board furthest from learner.	
7. Grasp throat piece edge closest to learner with thumb in opposition to fingers.	7. "Tighter"
8. Position thumb to the left of the lines on the jig.	8. Align center mark on tip clamp with center mark on the racquet. Verbalize "Match the lines."
9. Hold racquet tightly on jig by closing grip formed by fingertips and thumb.	
10. Release H_1.	
11. Pick up grease pencil with H_1.	
12. Make a mark on the top of the tip end of the racquet with grease pencil, connecting the existing lines of the jig.	
13. Make a mark on the top of the throat piece of the racquet with grease pencil, connecting the existing lines of the jig.	13. Align center mark on throat clamp with center mark on the racquet. Verbalize "Match the lines."
14. Release pencil.	
15. Remove H_2.	

FORMAT
Total Task

SUGGESTED HIERARCHY OF ASSISTS
Refer to Task Analysis 1, Job Station I

DEMONSTRATION INFORMATION
The trainer will demonstrate the entire task twice. The trainer will then remove the racquet from the jig and motion to the learner to begin.

GENERAL STRATEGIES FOR INFORMING
N/A

STRATEGIES FOR MOTIVATING
N/A

OTHER INFORMATION
N/A

TASK NAME
Placing the Racquet in the Stringing Machine— T.A. 3 (Job Station II)
PURPOSE
Same as above
CRITERION
I — Three correct consecutive trials without error or assistance
II — Three correct consecutive trials without error or assistance at the work station located in the sheltered workshop
MATERIALS
One unstrung racquet
TOOLS
N/A
EQUIPMENT
One Ektalon D racquet-stringing machine

TRAINING SET-UP (Diagram)
N/A

TRAINING SET-UP (Narrative)
Location of Learner in Relation to Task
The learner will be standing in front of the Ektalon D stringing machine
Position of Trainer in Relation to Learner
The trainer will be to the right of the learner.
Description of Environmental Setting
The setting is the same as in Task Analysis 2.

ADDITIONAL INTRODUCTORY INFORMATION
N/A

Task Name	Locating Center Holes on Racquet Using the Centering Jig — T.A. 2 (Job Station II)	MG&A

Learner Description Trainer Advisor	Agency Sheet 10 of 48 Total Training Time (minutes) _____ Criterion

Trials	Date	Place H₁	Hold jig	Position H₂	Slide	Release H₂	Place H₂	Grasp	Position	Hold	Release H₁	Pick up H₁	Mark	Mark	Release pencil	Remove H₂													Errors	Trial Time	Comments
1																															
2																															
3																															
4																															
5																															
6																															
7																															
8																															
9																															
0																															
1																															
2																															
3																															
4																															
5																															
6																															
7																															
8																															
9																															
0																															

FORMAT
Total Task

SUGGESTED HIERARCHY OF ASSISTS
Refer to Task Analysis 1

DEMONSTRATION INFORMATION
The trainer will demonstrate the task twice and then motion to the learner to begin.

GENERAL STRATEGIES FOR INFORMING
N/A

STRATEGIES FOR MOTIVATING
N/A

OTHER INFORMATION
This Task Analysis is the same as Task Analysis 2 except for the marking of the center points.
If more power or step specification is required, please refer to Task Analysis 2.

CONTENT TASK ANALYSIS (Learner Action)	SPECIFIC INFORMING STRATEGIES (Trainer Action)
1. Insert racquet into stringing machine.	
2. Center racquet tip.	2. "Match the lines."
3. Tighten clamp.	
4. Center racquet's throat.	4. "Match the lines."
5. Tighten clamp.	

TASK NAME
Positioning the Racquet — T.A. 4 (Job Station II)
PURPOSE
Same as above
CRITERION
I — Three correct consecutive trials without error or assistance
II — Three correct consecutive trials without error or assistance at the work station located in the sheltered workshop
MATERIALS
Unstrung Ektalon racquets
TOOLS
N/A
EQUIPMENT
One centering jig; one Ektalon D racquet-stringing machine

TRAINING SET-UP (Diagram)
N/A

TRAINING SET-UP (Narrative)
Location of Learner in Relation to Task
The learner begins by sitting at the work table where the centering jig is located. The learner moves between the work table and stringing machine.
Position of Trainer in Relation to Learner
The trainer is standing in back of the learner when the learner is at the work table and to the right of the learner when the learner is working with the stringing machine.
Description of Environmental Setting
The setting is the same as in Task Analysis 2.

ADDITIONAL INTRODUCTORY INFORMATION
N/A

Task Name	Placing the Racquet in the Stringing Machine — T.A. 3 (Job Station II)	MG&A

Learner Description Trainer Advisor	Agency Sheet __14__ of __48__ Total Training Time (minutes) _____ Criterion

Trials	Date	Insert	Center	Tighten	Center	Tighten																								Errors	Trial Time	Comments
1																																
2																																
3																																
4																																
5																																
6																																
7																																
8																																
9																																
0																																
1																																
2																																
3																																
4																																
5																																
6																																
7																																
8																																
9																																
0																																

FORMAT
Total Task

SUGGESTED HIERARCHY OF ASSISTS
Refer to Task Analysis 1

DEMONSTRATION INFORMATION
The trainer will demonstrate the task once and then motion to the learner to begin.

GENERAL STRATEGIES FOR INFORMING
N/A

STRATEGIES FOR MOTIVATING
N/A

OTHER INFORMATION
N/A

CONTENT TASK ANALYSIS (Learner Action)	SPECIFIC INFORMING STRATEGIES (Trainer Action)

1. Visually check inside of racquet to make sure all eyelets are in place, that is, none are missing.
2. Place pointer finger H_1 on inside of racquet rim.
3. Circle the entire racquet to check that all eyelets are in place.
4. Replace racquet if eyelet(s) are missing.
5. Find center of racquet by using jig.
6. Grasp racquet handle in left hand.
7. Pincer grasp tip of racquet with right hand.
8. Pass the left side of the racquet head through the throat clamp.
9. Position tip of lower lip of the tip clamp.
10. Position throat on lower lip of the throat clamp.
11. Center the racquet on the lower lip of the tip clamp.
12. Position thumb and index fingers of left hand on either side of tip clamp.
13. Hold securely into position with left hand.
14. Swing upper tip clamp into position with right hand.
15. Tighten tip clamp by turning tip knob screw clockwise with right hand.
16. Center the racquet on the lower lip of the throat clamp.
17. Hold racquet securely in position with left hand.
18. Tighten throat clamp by turning throat knot screw clockwise with right hand.

TASK NAME
Preparing the String — T.A. 5 (Job Station III)
PURPOSE
Same as above
CRITERION
I — Three correct consecutive trials without error or assistance
II — Three correct consecutive trials without error or assistance at the work station located in the sheltered workshop
MATERIALS
Bag of string, 25' lengths
TOOLS
Dyke wire cutters
EQUIPMENT
N/A

TRAINING SET-UP (Diagram)
N/A

TRAINING SET-UP (Narrative)
Location of Learner in Relation to Task
The learner will be standing in front of a work table. A box of racquet strings is on the table.
Position of Trainer in Relation to Learner
The trainer will be standing to the right of the learner.
Description of Environmental Setting
The training will take place at the work station located in the sheltered workshop.

ADDITIONAL INTRODUCTORY INFORMATION
The dyke wire cutters are placed to the left of the box of string. This is the "out-of-use" position.

Task Name Positioning the Racquet — T.A. 4 (Job Station II) **MG&A**

Learner
Description
Trainer
Advisor

Agency
Sheet 18 **of** 48
Total Training Time (minutes) _____
Criterion

Trials	Date	Visual check	Place finger H₁	Circle	Replace or skip step	Find center	Grasp	Pincer grasp	Pass	Position	Position	Center	Position	Hold	Swing	Tighten	Center	Hold	Tighten	Errors	Trial Time	Comments
1																						
2																						
3																						
4																						
5																						
6																						
7																						
8																						
9																						
0																						
1																						
2																						
3																						
4																						
5																						
6																						
7																						
8																						
9																						
0																						

CONTENT TASK ANALYSIS (Learner Action)	SPECIFIC INFORMING STRATEGIES (Trainer Action)
1. Remove racquet string from package.	
2. Pincer grasp one string with H_1.	
3. Shake string to uncoil.	
4. Pincer grasp one end of string with H_2.	
5. Encircle string next to H_2 with H_1 with light palmar grasp.	
6. GREM (Grasp with Repeated Extension Method)	
a. Full extension of H_2 from H_2 side of body.	
b. Allow string to slide through H_1.	
c. Grasp string at H_1 with remaining fingers.	
d. Repeat a, b, and c until end of string is reached.	
7. Pincer grasp remaining end of string with H_1.	
8. Release three-finger grasp of H_2.	
9. Match ends of string.	
10. Pincer grasp ends of H_2.	
11. Repeat Steps 5–7 to find center of string (folded end) forming a loop.	
12. Release string from H_2.	12. "Match the lines."
13. Pincer grasp string (making a 3" loop) with H_2.	
14. Release H_1.	
15. Grasp dykes (cutting tool) with H_1.	
16. Insert string of loop into jaws of dyke with H_2.	
17. Hold strings taut with H_2.	
18. Cut loop.	
19. Return dykes to tool tray casting.	
20. Pincer grasp one string end with H_2.	20. "Hold string tighter."
21. Release second string from H_1, allowing it to drop on floor.	
22. Wind string held by H_2 around H_2 palm with H_1.	
23. Replace wound string into package.	
24. Return package to tool tray casting.	

FORMAT
Total Task

SUGGESTED HIERARCHY OF ASSISTS
Refer to Task Analysis 1

DEMONSTRATION INFORMATION
The trainer will demonstrate the task twice using the following procedure

Part	Manipulation	Verbalization
Package	Open	
String	Uncoil	
String	GREM to match ends	"Match the ends."
String	GREM to make loops	
Dykes	Position	
String	Pull taut	"Hold string tight."
Dykes	Cut string	
String	Coil	
String	Replace in package	"Good"

GENERAL STRATEGIES FOR INFORMING
N/A

STRATEGIES FOR MOTIVATING
N/A

OTHER INFORMATION
N/A

TASK NAME
Stringing the Mainstrings — T.A. 6 (Job Station IV)
PURPOSE
Same as above
CRITERION
I — Three correct consecutive trials without error or assistance
II — Three correct consecutive trials without error or assistance at the work station located in the sheltered workshop
MATERIALS
Ektalon racquetball racquets; string in ½' lengths
TOOLS
N/A
EQUIPMENT
Ektalon Model D racquet stringer
TRAINING SET-UP (Diagram)
N/A

TRAINING SET-UP (Narrative)
Location of Learner in Relation to Task
The learner will be standing directly in front of a box of string.
Position of Trainer in Relation to Learner
The trainer will be standing to the right of the learner.
Description of Environmental Setting
Training will take place in an isolated room with adequate lighting for fine visual work.

ADDITIONAL INTRODUCTORY INFORMATION
N/A

Task Name Preparing the String — T.A. 5 (Job Station III)   MG&A

Learner
Description
Trainer
Advisor

Agency
Sheet _22_ of _48_
Total Training Time (minutes) _____
Criterion

Trials / Date / Remove / Pincer H₁ / Shake / Pincer H₁ / Encircle / GREM / Pincer H₁ / Release H₂ / Match ends / Pincer H₁ / Repeat 5–7 / Release H₂ / Pincer H₁ / Release H₁ / Grasp dykes / Insert H₂ / Hold H₂ / Cut loop / Return / Pincer H₁ / Release 2nd string / Wind / Replace / Return / Errors / Trial Time / Comments

(blank data grid rows 1–0)

CONTENT TASK ANALYSIS (Learner Action)	SPECIFIC INFORMING STRATEGIES (Trainer Action)
1. Pick up string from floor.	
2. Pincer grasp H_2 one end of string.	
3. Encircle strand with light palmar grasp in H_1.	
4.* Perform GREM procedure.	
5. Pincer grasp remaining end of string with H_1.	
6. Release three-finger grasp of H_2.	
7. Match ends of strings.	
8. Pincer grasp ends with H_2.	
9. Repeat steps.	
10. Pincer grasp strands approximately 2" from end with H_2.	
11. Position self at Ektalon machine.	
12. Rotate stand until tip clamp points toward learner.	
13. Pincer grasp H_1 side strand with H_1, approximately 2" from end.	
14. Insert string through eyelet 22 of H_1 side with H_1.	14. "Next to line"
15. Insert string through eyelet 22 of H_2 side with H_2.	15. "Next to line"
16. Pincer grasp both strings with H_2 on outside of racquet while releasing H_1.	
17. Pincer grasp strings inside of racquet frame with H_1.	
18. Release H_2.	
19. Pull both strings to throat clamp with H_1.	
20. Release H_1.	
21. Pincer grasp the H_1 side string approximately 2" from end with H_1.	
22. Insert string through throat eyelet 7 on H_1 side with H_1.	
23. Extend string end through the throat on the open side of the throat clamp with H_1.	

(CONTINUED)

CONTENT TASK ANALYSIS (Learner Action)	SPECIFIC INFORMING STRATEGIES (Trainer Action)
24. Release H_1.	
25. Pincer grasp end of H_1 string with H_1.	
26. Extend string approximately 1" beyond throat piece.	
27. Release H_1.	
28. Pincer grasp H_2 side string approximately 2" from end with H_1.	
29. Repeat Steps 19–24 for H_2 side.	
30. Rotate machine 180°.	
31. Pincer grasp string ends with H_2.	
32. Match string ends.	
33. Pull strings taut repeating GREM procedure.	
34. Release H_2 maintaining tautness with H_1.	
35. Release H_1.	

*For the complete GREM procedure refer to "Preparing the String" Task Analysis.

Task Name — Stringing the Mainstrings — T.A. 6 (Job Station IV)   MG&A

Learner	
Description	Agency
Trainer	Sheet 27 of 48
Advisor	Total Training Time (minutes) _____
	Criterion

Trials	Date	Pick up	Pincer H₂	Encircle	GREM	Pincer	Release	Match ends	Pincer H₂	Repeat	Pincer H₂	Position	Rotate	Pincer H₁	Insert	Insert	Pincer H₂	Pincer H₁	Release H₂	Pull	Release H₁	Pincer H₁	Insert	Extend	Release H₁	Pincer H₁	Extend string	Release H₁	Repeat 19-24	Rotate 180°	Pincer H₂	Match ends	Pull	Release H₂	Release H₁			Errors	Trial Time	Comments
1																																								
2																																								
3																																								
4																																								
5																																								
6																																								
7																																								
8																																								
9																																								
0																																								
1																																								
2																																								
3																																								
4																																								
5																																								
6																																								
7																																								
8																																								
9																																								
0																																								

FORMAT
Total Task

SUGGESTED HIERARCHY OF ASSISTS
Refer to Task Analysis 1

DEMONSTRATION INFORMATION
The trainer will demonstrate the following procedure twice.

Part	Manipulation	Verbalization
String	Match ends	
String	Insert ends into eyelets 22	"Insert string next to line."
String	Insert ends into eyelets	"Insert string next to line."
String	Match ends; pull taut	
Clamp	Position wrong	"Try another place."
	right	"Good"
Tensioner	Tension	"Good"

Following this procedure the trainer will motion to the learner to begin.

GENERAL STRATEGIES FOR INFORMING
N/A

STRATEGIES FOR MOTIVATING
N/A

OTHER INFORMATION
N/A

CONTENT TASK ANALYSIS (Learner Action)	SPECIFIC INFORMING STRATEGIES (Trainer Action)
1. Pincer grasp H$_1$-side string clamp below lever with H$_1$.	
2. Glide clamp to center of glide bar.	
3. Rotate string clamp until jaws of clamp are beneath H$_1$ string.	
4. Position clamp perpendicular to frame table encasing H$_1$ string in jaws.	
5. Glide clamp within finger width of tip clamp.	
6. Hold grasp.	
7. Place thumb H$_1$ on lever.	
8. Press lever toward clamp until it locks into position.	
9. Release H$_1$.	
10. Release clamped string from H$_2$.	
11. Palmar grasp held string between H$_2$ and racquet with H$_1$.	
12. Locate end of string.	
13. Pincer grasp string approximately 4″ from the end with H$_1$.	
14. Insert string through the next throat eyelet (6) from outside of racquet.	
15. Release H$_2$.	
16. Pincer grasp end of string with H$_2$.	
17. Extend string to tip clamp.	
18. Release H$_1$.	
19. Pincer grasp string 2″ from end with H$_1$.	
20. Insert string through next tip eyelet (21) on H$_2$ side of racquet from inside of rim, making sure string passes on outside of tip clamp stirrup.	
21. Release H$_2$.	
22. Reach over tip clamp with H$_2$.	
23. Pincer grasp end of string H$_2$.	
24. Pull toward learner, allowing machine to rotate freely.	
25. Pull string taut using GREM.	

(CONTINUED)

TASK NAME
Tensioning the Mainstrings — T.A. 7 (Job Station IV)
PURPOSE
Same as above
CRITERION
I — Three correct consecutive trials without error or assistance
II — Three correct consecutive trials without error or assistance at the work station located in the sheltered workshop
MATERIALS
Ektalon racquetball racquets; string in 12½′ lengths
TOOLS
N/A
EQUIPMENT
Ektalon Model D racquet stringer

TRAINING SET-UP (Diagram)
N/A

TRAINING SET-UP (Narrative)
Location of Learner in Relation to Task
The learner will be standing directly in front of the racquet-stringing machine.
Position of Trainer in Relation to Learner
The trainer will be standing to the right of the learner.
Description of Environmental Setting
Training will take place in an isolated room with adequate lighting for fine visual work.

ADDITIONAL INTRODUCTORY INFORMATION
N/A

CONTENT TASK ANALYSIS (Learner Action)	SPECIFIC INFORMING STRATEGIES (Trainer Action)
26. Grasp string near tip clamp with right hand.	
27. Grasp crank knob on tensioning assembly with left hand.	
28. Rotate crank counter clockwise until tensioning assembly is within 3″.	
29. Insert string in self-tightening clamp, keeping taut.	
30. Pull string downward lightly.	
31. Rotate crank clockwise until automatic lock lever springs out.	
32. Release both hands.	
33. Position unattached string clamp for opposite side by repeating step, changing sides where necessary.	
34. Pincer grasp clamp arm with fingertips of right hand with right thumb.	
35. Grasp string behind self-tensioning clamp and lift string out with right hand.	
36. Grasp and rotate crank clockwise until tensioning assembly reaches end of tensioning arm with left hand.	
37. Release left hand.	
38. Replace right hand grasp with H₂.	
39. Stringing: Locate end of string.	
40. Pincer grasp string approximately 2″ from end with H₁.	
41. Insert string through the next tip eyelet on last tensioned side with H₁.	
42. Release H₂.	
43. Pincer grasp string end inside rim with H₂.	
44. Extend H₂ to throat clamp.	
45. Pincer grasp string approximately 2″ from end with H₁.	
46. Release H₂.	
47. Insert string through next throat eyelet on last tensioned side with H₁, making sure string rests above throat rim.	

(CONTINUED)

CONTENT TASK ANALYSIS (Learner Action)	SPECIFIC INFORMING STRATEGIES (Trainer Action)
48. Reach over throat clamp with H₂.	
49. Pincer grasp end of string H₂.	
50. Release H₁ while pulling string toward learner with H₂.	
51. Lightly palmar grasp string between H₂ and racquet with H₁.	
52. Pull string taut using GREM as described in Step 7, allowing machine to rotate.	
53. Release H₁ and grasp string near throat clamp with H₁.	
54. Release H₂.	
55. Grasp last used string clamp below the lever with H₁.	
56. Pull lever toward learner until jaws release with H₂.	
57. Slide clamp to center of glide bar.	
58. Pull clamp toward learner, tilting clamp allowing glide bar to lead until jaws are beneath last tensioned string.	
59. Position clamp perpendicular to frame table encasing just-tensioned string between jaws of clamp.	
60. Slide clamp toward tensioning assembly as far as it will go.	
61. Close string clamp by pressing lever toward clamp with H₂ or H₁ thumb until it locks into position.	
62. Release both hands.	
63. Continue stringing the racquet from throat to top to throat by repeating Steps 16–24 until top eyelet 15 has been strung and the string secured with the string clamp. The tension should be released.	
64. Grasp string on unstrung side with H₂.	
65. Tension string by repeating Steps 27–31.	
66. Reposition clamp by repeating Steps 1–8.	
67. Release tension by repeating Steps 34–36.	
68. Continue stringing this side of the racquet by repeating these steps.	

(CONTINUED)

FORMAT
Total Task

SUGGESTED HIERARCHY OF ASSISTS
Refer to Task Analysis 1

DEMONSTRATION INFORMATION
N/A

GENERAL STRATEGIES FOR INFORMING
N/A

STRATEGIES FOR MOTIVATING
N/A

OTHER INFORMATION
Training will begin without a demonstration. The trainer will provide guidance through the entire task until the learner has picked up enough information to work primarily on his own.

CONTENT TASK ANALYSIS (Learner Action)	SPECIFIC INFORMING STRATEGIES (Trainer Action)
Remove both string clamps by:	
69. Repeat Steps 56–57.	
70. Pull clamp toward learner, tilting clamp and allowing slide bar to lead until glide bar glides are off rail slots. Use H_2 to assist if necessary.	
71. Place glide bar with string clamp to the side.	
Mounting clamp for cross string:	
72. Position body at tip of clamp.	
73. Pass glide bar between racquet and frame table.	
74. Grasp bar end piece with thumb of H_1, position in line with bar and index finger aligned with thumb, fingers grasping lower edge.	
75. Lower assembly until string clamp rests on frame table.	
76. With H_2, grasp H_2 end piece similarly to H_1.	

Task Name — Tensioning the Mainstrings (continued)

Learner
Description
Trainer
Advisor

Agency
Sheet 35 of 48
Total Training Time (minutes) _____
Criterion

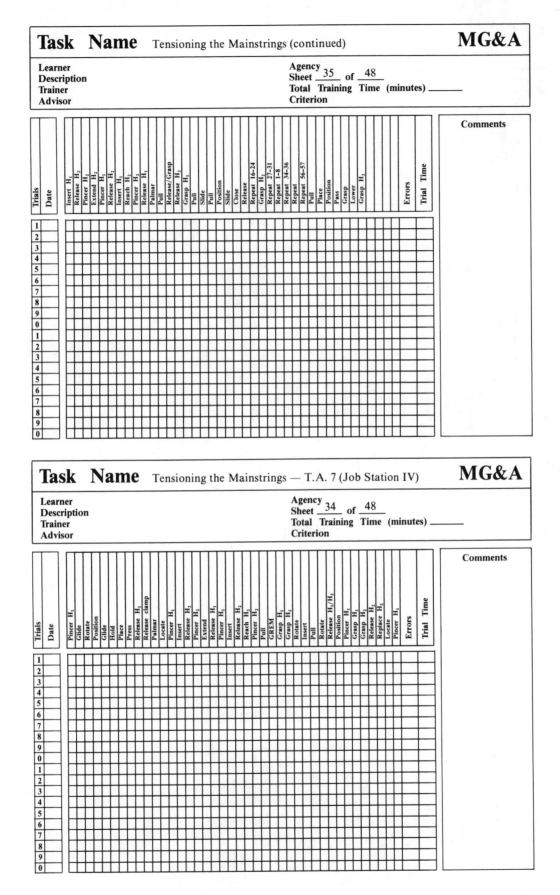

Trials	Date	Insert H₁	Release H₂	Pincer H₂	Extend H₂	Pincer H₁	Release H₂	Insert H₁	Reach H₂	Pincer H₂	Release H₁	Palmar	Pull	Release/Grasp	Release H₂	Grasp H₁	Pull	Slide	Pull	Position	Slide	Close	Release	Repeat 16–24	Grasp H₂	Repeat 27–31	Repeat 1–8	Repeat 34–36	Repeat	Repeat 56–57	Pull	Place	Position	Pass	Grasp	Lower	Grasp H₂	Errors	Trial Time	Comments
1																																								
2																																								
3																																								
4																																								
5																																								
6																																								
7																																								
8																																								
9																																								
0																																								
1																																								
2																																								
3																																								
4																																								
5																																								
6																																								
7																																								
8																																								
9																																								
0																																								

Task Name — Tensioning the Mainstrings — T.A. 7 (Job Station IV)

MG&A

Learner
Description
Trainer
Advisor

Agency
Sheet 34 of 48
Total Training Time (minutes) _____
Criterion

Trials	Date	Pincer H₁	Glide	Rotate	Position	Glide	Hold	Place	Press	Release H₁	Release clamp	Palmar	Locate	Pincer H₁	Insert	Release H₂	Pincer H₂	Extend	Release H₁	Pincer H₁	Insert	Release H₂	Reach H₂	Pincer H₂	Pull	GREM	Grasp H₁	Grasp H₂	Rotate	Insert	Pull	Rotate	Release H₁/H₂	Position	Pincer H₁	Grasp H₂	Grasp H₂	Release H₂	Replace H₂	Locate	Pincer H₁	Errors	Trial Time	Comments
1																																												
2																																												
3																																												
4																																												
5																																												
6																																												
7																																												
8																																												
9																																												
0																																												
1																																												
2																																												
3																																												
4																																												
5																																												
6																																												
7																																												
8																																												
9																																												
0																																												

TASK NAME
Knot Tying — T.A. 8 (Job Station V)
PURPOSE
Same as above
CRITERION
I — Three correct consecutive trials without error or assistance
II — Three correct consecutive trials without error or assistance located at the work station in the sheltered workshop
MATERIALS
Ektalon racquetball racquet, string woven
TOOLS
Dyke cutters, needlenose pliers
EQUIPMENT
Ektalon Model D stringing machine

TRAINING SET-UP (Diagram)
N/A

TRAINING SET-UP (Narrative)
Location of Learner in Relation to Task
The learner will be standing directly in front of the stringing machine.
Position of Trainer in Relation to Learner
The trainer will be standing to the right of the learner.
Description of Environmental Setting
Training will take place in an isolated room with adequate lighting for fine visual work.

ADDITIONAL INTRODUCTORY INFORMATION
There is a tool tray attached to the stringing machine. The dykes and needlenose pliers are in the "out-of-use" position when placed on this tray.

CONTENT TASK ANALYSIS (Learner Action)	SPECIFIC INFORMING STRATEGIES (Trainer Action)
1. Grasp string 2" from end with H_1.	
2. Insert string through proper eyelet. (For mainstrings and throat cross string tie knot on 4th string and for tip cross tie knot on 5th string in from outside.)	
3. Pincer grasp string end with H_2.	
4. Pull string taut while releasing H_1.	
5. Insert string downward on the tip clamp side of the anchor string with H_2.	
6. Pincer grasp string end underneath racquet with H_1.	
7. Pull string down with H_1 while H_2 fingers catch loop above racquet.	
8. Maintain a loop.	8. "Hold loop straight."
9. Insert string end up on the outer side of the anchor string with H_1.	
10. Insert string end through loop while releasing loop from H_2.	
11. Pincer grasp the string end with H_2.	
12. Pull string several inches with H_2 while H_1 maintains a loop beneath the racquet.	
13. Bring string over first loop with H_2.	
14. Insert string down on outer side of the anchor string.	
15. Make sure string end goes through loop held in H_1.	
16. Release H_1.	
17. Firmly grasp string end with H_1.	
18. Grasp loop presently held in H_2.	18. "Hold loop straight."
19. Pull loop up and toward learner until taut, allowing string to slide through grasp in H_2.	
20. Release H_1 and H_2.	
21. Pick up knot-securing tool with H_1 and pliers in H_2.	
22. Encase anchor string with knot-securing tool close to knot with H_1 from beneath racquet.	
23. Place thumb of H_1 on outer rim of racquet.	
24. Tighten knot by pulling upward on loop with pliers in H_2.	
25. Secure knot against rim of racquet with knot securing tool in H_1.	25. "Hold pliers tight."

(CONTINUED)

CONTENT TASK ANALYSIS (Learner Action)	SPECIFIC INFORMING STRATEGIES (Trainer Action)
26. Release pliers from loop above racquet.	
27. While holding pliers in palm of H_2, position beneath the racquet.	
28. Grasp string end.	
29. Grasp end of string and pull inward until taut with H_2.	
30. Release dykes; bring string up on same side of knot with H_1.	
31. With pliers, firmly grasp string just above racquet rim and pull upward with H_2; release pliers; tighten knot while palm of H_2 presses downward on racquet.	
32. With H_2, bring string end up between strings 17 and 18.	
33. Release pliers and return to tool tray casting. Pick up pliers with H_1.	
34. With H_1, pick up dykes.	
35. Retighten with pliers; grasp string between hand and racquet.	
36. With dykes, cut string ⅛th to ¼th" from knot. Release H_2.	
37. Return dykes to tool tray casting. Pull string taut.	
38. Remove clamp from table.	

FORMAT
Total Task

SUGGESTED HIERARCHY OF ASSISTS
Refer to Task Analysis 1

DEMONSTRATION INFORMATION
N/A

GENERAL STRATEGIES FOR INFORMING
N/A

STRATEGIES FOR MOTIVATING
N/A

OTHER INFORMATION
Knot tying will initially require direct hand manipulation through entire task. A demonstration will not be given.

TASK NAME
Waxing and Stringing Cross Strings — T.A. 9 (Job Station VI)

PURPOSE
Same as above

CRITERION
I — There are five different stations in this analysis. Criterion for each station is three consecutive trials without error or assistance. Criterion for the complete Task Analysis, that is, all five stations, is two complete consecutive trials of all stations without error or assistance.

II — Two complete consecutive trials without error or assistance at the work station located in the sheltered workshop.

MATERIALS
String in 12½′ lengths; string in 1′ lengths and color-coded bees' wax; unstrung Ektalon racquetball racquet; Ektalon racquet with mainstrings strung

TOOLS
Dyke cutters; needlenose pliers

EQUIPMENT
Ektalon Model D racquetball stringing machine

TRAINING SET-UP (Diagram)
N/A

TRAINING SET-UP (Narrative)
Location of Learner in Relation to Task
The learner will be sitting at a table for simulated Job Stations 1–5. When working with the stringing machine he will be standing directly in front of the machine.

Position of Trainer in Relation to Learner
In all cases the trainer will be positioned to the right of the learner.

Description of Environmental Setting
Training will take place in an isolated room with adequate lighting for fine visual work. The five job stations are set in chronological order. The stringing machine is positioned after Station 5.

ADDITIONAL INTRODUCTORY INFORMATION
This analysis has two main components. The first component requires the learner to complete five simulated stages of waxing and weaving cross strings. Following criterion of this first component, the learner is moved to the Ektalon stringing machine. The color-coded cross strings are not used under this condition. All strings are the same color.

Task Name Knot Tying — T.A. 8 (Job Station V) MG&A

Learner	Agency
Description	Sheet 40 of 48
Trainer	Total Training Time (minutes) _____
Advisor	Criterion

Trials	Date	String end	Count 4	Insert	Pull taut	Down	Hold top loop	Up	Through loop	Pull end	Bottom loop	Down	Prep knot	Tools	Knot aide	Pliers pull	Aide press	Tighten	String end	Count 4	Insert	Pull taut	Down	Hold top loop	Up	Through loop	Pull end	Bottom loop	Down	Prep knot	Tools	Knot aide	Pliers pull	Aide press	Tighten	Errors	Trial Time	Comments
1																																						
2																																						
3																																						
4																																						
5																																						
6																																						
7																																						
8																																						
9																																						
0																																						
1																																						
2																																						
3																																						
4																																						
5																																						
6																																						
7																																						
8																																						
9																																						
0																																						

CONTENT TASK ANALYSIS (Learner Action)	SPECIFIC INFORMING STRATEGIES (Trainer Action)
1. Pick up block of wax with H_1.	
2. Starting on H_1 side of racquet, rub wax from tip to throat of racquet in direction main strings are strung.	
3. Continue Step 2 until all strings are waxed.	
4. Replace wax in tool tray.	
5. Position string clamp on machine, if necessary, by following mounting procedure.	
6. Remove other half of string from package.	
7. Uncoil string by shaking.	
8. Pincer grasp string 2" from end with H_1.	
9. Insert string in tip eyelet 18 on H_1 side from the outside of the racquet.	
10. Pass string over main string from tip eyelet 19.	10. "Insert here."
11. Release H_1.	
12. Pincer grasp string inside racquet frame with H_1.	
13. Pull about 2½' of string through eyelet.	
14. Insert string down between strings from eyelet 19 and 20 with H_1.	
15. Pincer grasp string beneath racquet with H_2.	
16. Release H_1.	16. "Weave under."
17. Insert up between strings from eyelets 20 and 21 with H_2.	
18. Pincer grasp string above racquet frame with H_1.	
19. Extend H_1 upward pulling entire loop through.	
20. Continue this weaving pattern until string is held in H_1 above racquet between eyelets 18 and 19 on H_2 side.	
21. Insert string through eyelet 18 on H_2 side from inside of racquet with H_1 (assistance with H_2 may be necessary).	
22. Grasp string on outside of racquet frame with H_2.	
23. Pull entire loop through 2½ feet.	
24. Insert string into eyelet 19 on H_2 side from outside racquet frame with H_2.	
25. Pass string beneath string from eyelet 20.	
26. Pincer grasp string with H_1 while releasing H_2.	
27. Insert string upward between strings from eyelets 20 and 21.	

(CONTINUED)

CONTENT TASK ANALYSIS (Learner Action)	SPECIFIC INFORMING STRATEGIES (Trainer Action)
28. Pass string between tip of frame and first cross string.	
29. Pincer grasp end of string above racquet frame with H_2.	
30. Pull upward leaving a 6" loop on outside frame.	30. "Insert here."
31. Insert string down between strings from eyelets 21 and 22 with H_2.	
32. Pass string between tip of frame and first cross string.	
33. Pincer grasp string below racquet with H_1.	
34. Continue this weaving pattern until string is held in H_2 above racquet frame between strings from eyelets 21 and 22 on H_1 side.	
35. Insert string through eyelet 19 on H_1 side from inside of racquet frame with H_2.	
36. Pincer grasp end of string with H_1.	
37. Pull string through leaving 6" loop on H_2 side.	
38. Insert string through eyelet 20 on H_1 side from outside of rim with H_1.	
39. Pincer grasp string end and pull taut with H_2.	
40. Tie knot around string from eyelet 20 on H_1 side by following knot procedure (Re: Job Station IV).	
41. Tension loop from tip eyelet 19 on H_2 side by following tension procedure Steps 31 through 41 (JS IV).	
42. Position string clamp on cross string tensioned in last step by following tensioning procedure Steps 5–13 (JS IV).	
43. Release tension following tensioning procedure, Steps 34–38 (JS IV).	
44. Tension string from tip eyelet 18 on H_1 side by following tensioning Steps 31–41 (JS IV).	
45. Position string clamp by following procedure Steps 5–13 (JS IV).	
46. Release tension by following procedure Steps 38–42 (JS IV).	
47. Locate end of string.	
48. With H_1, pincer grasp string approximately 1" from end.	
49. With H_1, insert string through next eyelet.	

(CONTINUED)

CONTENT TASK ANALYSIS (Learner Action) | SPECIFIC INFORMING STRATEGIES (Trainer Action)

50. With H$_2$ pincer grasp end of string and pull approximately 1½ feet of string through eyelet.
51. Switch end of string into H$_1$.
52. With H$_1$, insert end of string down between mainstrings from eyelets 18 and 19.
53. With H$_2$, grasp end of string between racquet while releasing H$_1$.
54. With H$_2$, insert end of string up between mainstrings from eyelets 19 and 20.
55. With H$_1$, pincer grasp end of string above racquet and pull 1½ feet taut.
56. Continue weaving pattern until you reach eyelet 17 with H$_1$.
57. With H$_1$, insert string through next eyelet, 17.
58. With H$_2$, pincer grasp end of string and pull all of the string through the eyelet using a hand-over-hand method of pulling until all string is taut.
59. Tension string from eyelet 17.
60. Reposition clamp.
61. Release tension.
62. Repeat cross stringing the racquet in this manner by repeating stringing Step 48, and 47, 51, and 49 until tip eyelet 1 is reached.
63. String tip eyelet 1 to tip eyelet 1 by starting under the mainstring from eyelet 19.
64. Repeat Steps 47, 51, and 49.
65. String throat eyelet 1 to throat eyelet 1 by starting over mainstring from eyelet 19.
66. Repeat Steps 47, 51, and 49.
67. String throat eyelet 2 to throat eyelet 2 by starting under mainstring from eyelet 20.
68. Repeat Steps 47, 51, and 49.
69. With H$_1$, insert end of string through throat eyelet 3 on H$_2$ side (last clamp side) from outside of rim.
70. Pull string taut.
71. Secure string with knot around mainstring from eyelet 20 by repeating knot procedure.

FORMAT
Total Task: Each job station is taught individually using this format.

SUGGESTED HIERARCHY OF ASSISTS
Refer to Task Analysis 1

DEMONSTRATION INFORMATION
Each station is demonstrated twice. Use the following procedure for waxing.

Part	Manipulation	Verbalization
Wax	Waxing	—
String	Insert	"Start here."
String	GREM 2'	"Too much"
	Pull back 6"	"Good"
String	Weave	"Over; under"
String	Insert	—

GENERAL STRATEGIES FOR INFORMING
Every time the learner weaves in the wrong direction the trainer will: (1) stop learner; (2) require learner to verbalize over or under for five weaves following the error.

STRATEGIES FOR MOTIVATING
N/A

OTHER INFORMATION
Job Station Breakdowns

I — 1st mainstring
II — 3rd mainstring; consistent stringing of first three strings
III — 5th mainstring; visual check, vertically, of over and under strings
IV — Weaving entire racquet with color-coded string
V — Weaving entire racquet and changing the colors of the string to make sure learner understands concept

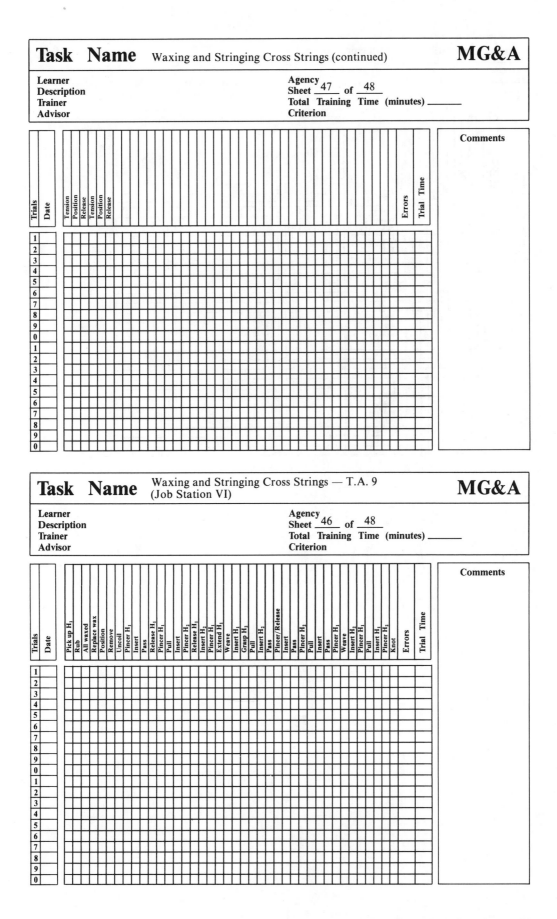

Task Name Waxing and Stringing Cross Strings (continued) **MG&A**

Learner	Agency
Description	Sheet 47 of 48
Trainer	Total Training Time (minutes) _____
Advisor	Criterion

Columns: Trials | Date | Tension | Position | Release | Tension | Position | Release | ... | Errors | Trial Time | Comments

Trials: 1 2 3 4 5 6 7 8 9 0 1 2 3 4 5 6 7 8 9 0

Task Name Waxing and Stringing Cross Strings — T.A. 9
(Job Station VI) **MG&A**

Learner	Agency
Description	Sheet 46 of 48
Trainer	Total Training Time (minutes) _____
Advisor	Criterion

Columns: Trials | Date | Pick up H₁ | Rub | All waxed | Replace wax | Position | Remove | Uncoil | Pincer H₁ | Insert | Pass | Release H₁ | Pincer H₁ | Pull | Insert | Pincer H₂ | Release H₁ | Insert H₂ | Pincer H₁ | Extend H₁ | Weave | Insert H₁ | Grasp H₂ | Pull | Insert H₁ | Pass | Pincer/Release | Insert | Pass | Pincer H₂ | Pull | Insert | Pass | Pincer H₁ | Weave | Insert H₂ | Pincer H₂ | Pull | Insert H₁ | Pincer H₂ | Knot | Errors | Trial Time | Comments

Trials: 1 2 3 4 5 6 7 8 9 0 1 2 3 4 5 6 7 8 9 0

Task Name — Stringing Cross Strings

MG&A

Learner
Description
Trainer
Advisor

Agency
Sheet __48__ of __48__
Total Training Time (minutes) _____
Criterion

Trials	Date	Cross string	String end	Locate 2	Insert 2	Weave o/u	Locate exit	Exit 2	Pull 1'	Locate 3	Insert 3	Pull taut	Knot	Tension K	Tension K		STRING NUMBERS																							Magnum	Knot	Tension K	Tension K	Straighten	Errors	Trial Time	Comments
																	1	2	3	4	5	6	7	8	9	10	11	12	13	14	15	16	17	18	19	20	21	22								
1																Tension																														
2																Clamp																														
3																Release																														
4																Insert																														
5																Begin																														
6																Weave o/u																														
7																Exit																														
8																Pull taut																														
9																Tension																														
10																Clamp																														
11																Release																														
12																Insert																														
13																Begin																														
14																Weave o/u																														
15																Exit																														
16																Pull taut																														
17																Tension																														
18																Clamp																														
19																Release																														
20																Insert																														
21																Begin																														
22																Weave o/u																														
23																Exit																														
24																Pull taut																														

SECTION 5

SERVICES AND RESOURCES

MARC GOLD & ASSOCIATES, INC.

Marc Gold & Associates, Inc. (MG&A) was incorporated in 1976 in order to provide a mechanism for governmental, private, and other organizations to gain access to the philosophy and training technology known as Try Another Way (TAW).

The activities of MG&A include the following:

1. Conducting two-day training conferences at which the philosophy of Try Another Way is explained and demonstrated.

2. Conducting or coordinating other professional conferences in related fields.

3. Providing a wide variety of training services, as described later.

4. Distributing task analyses, reports, books, manuals, sample contracts, etc.

5. Providing other individualized training activities or programs specifically designed at the request of an agency, organization, or individual.

In an effort to meet the needs of individuals and organizations desiring to be trained in Try Another Way, MG&A provides a number of programs ranging from short, introductory sessions to long-term extensive training programs. They are of three varieties:

1. Short sessions designed to inform people or expose them to the Try Another Way System
   Length — 1, 2, or 3 days
   Material covered — Overview of TAW, the TAW philosophy, task analysis, working relationships with clients, motivation, and other similar topics
   Maximum number — Unlimited, depending on capacity of room

2. Short-term training programs designed to provide initial training to people who desire to use the Try Another Way system with clients
   Length — 2, 3, 4 weeks
   Material covered — All overview material, plus basic training in writing task analyses and using those task analyses to train clients; using TAW instructional and motivational techniques
   Maximum number — Approximately 12 participants per trainer

3. Long-term training programs designed to provide comprehensive training in every aspect of the Try Another Way System. These programs are intended to bring participants to criterion as trainers of clients, and, in some cases, enable participants to reach criterion as trainers of trainers.
   Length — 1–5 years
   Material covered — All aspects of the TAW System
   Maximum number — Unlimited, depending on the number of MG&A coordinators used on the project

In addition, MG&A also contracts in the following areas:

1. Industrial technical consulting — These activities involve providing production-design changes, quality control and production monitoring improvements, and personnel training systems.

2. Workshop management services—Comprehensive endeavors in which MG&A assumes the role of workshop manager, organizes the shop in accordance with TAW specifications, secures contracts, trains staff, and operates the program until criterion is reached. Variations of this service provide similar activities without assuming the role of workshop manager.

3. Direct training and placement services for those labeled handicapped—Under this program, MG&A identifies potential industrial jobs, trains clients to assume those jobs, facilitates the integration of the workers, trains the existing staff to accommodate the new employees, and provides follow-up training as necessary.

If you are interested in activities or products described in this book, or if you are interested in pursuing ideas for training not described in this book, please contact one of the following MG&A offices.

Main Office

Marc Gold & Associates
P.O. Box 548
Ocean Springs, Mississippi 39564
(601) 875-8357
Mike Callahan, President

Texas Office

Marc Gold & Associates
P.O. Box 5100
Austin, Texas 78763
(512) 451-0879
Nancy Rhoads

Ohio Office

Marc Gold & Associates
5553 Crawford Drive
Columbus, Ohio 43229
(614) 846-7563
Bill Montooth

OTHER RESOURCES

Organizations and Firms

1. American Association on Mental Deficiency
   5101 Wisconsin Avenue N.W.
   Washington, D.C. 20016
   (800) 424-3688

   Professional organization for those who work with people who have been labeled mentally retarded or mentally deficient.

2. American Physical Therapy Association
   1156 15th Street N.W.
   Washington, D.C. 20005
   (202) 466-2080

   Professional organization for those in the field of physical therapy.

3. National Association for Retarded Citizens
   2709 Avenue E East
   Arlington, Texas 76011
   (817) 261-4961

Organization which provides referral information on state and local Association chapters; information regarding legislation and congressional action; an employer reimbursement program for on-the-job training; and research materials, publications, and bibliographies on all phases of mental retardation. List of available materials provided at no cost.

4. Bendix Corporation
Bicycle & Ignition Components Division
401 Bendix Drive
P. O. Box 4001
South Bend, Indiana 46634

Company which sells the bicycle brakes used by Marc Gold in his research and demonstrations. Price $2.73/each, Model 76 coaster brake, assembled and greased, less trim parts (price subject to change).

5. Closer Look
National Information Center for Parents of Handicapped Children and Youth
P. O. Box 1492
Washington, D.C. 20013

A national advocacy and information group interested in issues related to the needs of various populations that have been labeled handicapped. A newsletter and information packets are available at no cost.

6. Minnesota Diversified Industries, An Affirmative Industry
666 Pelham Boulevard
St. Paul, Minnesota 55114
(612) 646-2711

A firm offering technical consultation and support regarding the establishment of an affirmative industry or the conversion to an affirmative industry. Materials and manuals also available.

7. National Rehabilitation Association
1522 K Street N.W., Suite 1120
Washington, D.C. 20005
(202) 659-2430

The professional organization for those working in the field of vocational rehabilitation.

8. Ogden Lindsley
Behavior Research Company
Box 3351
Kansas City, Kansas 66103

An individual offering, among other things, data collection forms developed in conjunction with his Precision Teaching System.

9. Project MORE
George Peabody College
Box 318
Nashville, Tennessee 37203

A group offering a number of specific task analyses, especially in the area of daily living skills, for people who find it difficult to learn.

10. Research Press
    2612 N. Mattis Avenue
    Champaign, Illinois 61820
    (217) 352-3273

    A publisher offering a comprehensive line of books and materials in the behavioral sciences.

11. The Association for the Severely Handicapped (TASH) (Formerly AAESPH)
    1600 West Armory Way
    Garden View Suite
    Seattle, Washington 98119
    (206) 283-5055

    A professional organization for those who work with people who have been labeled severely or profoundly handicapped.

12. The Council for Exceptional Children
    1920 Association Drive
    Reston, Virginia 22091
    (800) 336-3728

    A professional organization for those who work with people who have been labeled handicapped or who require special services. Also features a complete publishing division. A book which could be of special interest is: Gadow, Kenneth. *Children on Medication: A Primer for School Personnel,* CEC, 1979. Prices: $7.75 (non-CEC member); $6.50 (CEC member) (prices subject to change).

13. The National Institute on Mental Retardation
    Kinsman NIMR Building, York University Campus
    4700 Keele Street, Downsview (Toronto)
    Ontario, Canada, M3J 1P3
    (416) 661-9611

    An organization sponsored by the Canadian Association for the Mentally Retarded. Offers material, literature, and training sessions related to topics in the field of mental retardation.

14. Lott Industries
    Larc Lane Plant
    Toledo, Ohio 43614
    (419) 385-4686

    A company manufacturing and selling training boards. Boards have five-ply mahogany-veneered backs and fronts with 18 three-ply mahogany-veneered adjustable dividers inside. Feature soft leather carrying straps and removable hinge pins, and unfold to 38½ x 14½. Price: $50 (price subject to change).

Films

1. People First
   The organization: People First
   P. O. Box 12642
   Salem, Oregon 97309
   (513) 362-0336

   A self-advocacy organization for people labeled developmentally disabled, providing opportunities to talk, solve problems, and make decisions. The organization also plans "People First" conferences for themselves and others.

   The film: James Stanfield Film Associates
   P. O. Box 1983
   Santa Monica, California 90406
   (213) 395-7466

   "People First" and other films relating to populations labeled handicapped are available for purchase and rental.

2. Film Productions of Indianapolis
   128 East 36th Street
   Indianapolis, Indiana 46205
   (317) 924-5163

   A firm which markets the film "Try Another Way" and the seven films in the Try Another Way Series. For any information regarding the sale or rental of the films, please contact Film Productions of Indianapolis. The following is a list of the films by title (or number) with a short annotation and the running time for each. Individual films (1–7) are $225 each (price subject to change).

   "Try Another Way" (27 min.) — This introductory overview to the Try Another Way System features Dr. Marc Gold explaining the concepts included in the approach, two training episodes, and two production episodes, as well as other information related to the use of Try Another Way.

   Film 1 — "Task Analysis: An Introduction to a Technology of Instruction" (18 min.)
   Dr. Gold shows the importance of the trainer's knowing the task he is to teach and being able to break it down into teachable components. Using different formats, Marc works with preschool children who are learning to build with blocks, to use screwdrivers, and to recognize coin values. Marc discusses Criterion, Data Collection, and the Seven-Phase Sequence for doing a complete Task Analysis.

   Film 2 — "Content and Process: Two Components of Task Analysis" (12 min.)
   How do you subdivide steps that are not teachable? In the second film Dr. Gold states, "'Teachable' is determined by the skills of the teacher and those of the learner." Marc trains two people learning to assemble electronic circuit boards, showing that though the subdivision of steps may be difficult for each person the result is the same. What do you do when a learner doesn't learn? In the answer to this question lies the real strength of his system.

Film 3 — "Formats for Single Pieces of Learning: Subcategories Of Process Task Analysis" (13 min.)

Match-to-sample? Oddity? Paired associate learning? How do you present the task? Marc explains these formats and demonstrates their use. He also covers recognition and recall, successive and simultaneous presentation. With demonstration and his unique whimsical style, Marc details the intricacies of teaching single pieces of learning.

Film 4 — "Formats for Multiple Pieces of Learning" (22 min.)

In this film Dr. Gold explains his bag of tricks and covers multiple pieces of learning: (1) forward chaining, (2) backward chaining, (3) total task presentation, and (4) organized exposure with feedback. He shows that much of what a person learns consists of pieces of information having logical connections to one another. As an example, the Total Task Presentation is demonstrated in the mobility training of a blind person with profound retardation.

Film 5 — "Feedback — General Issues" (20 min.)

"Feedback means letting the learner know what is wanted of him and if he is achieving it." Dr. Gold proceeds to explain the many facets of this concept in Film 5. Reinforcement and different types of feedback (concurrent, terminal, immediate, delayed, verbal, nonverbal) are discussed. Feedback is demonstrated by trainers working with deaf-blind children.

Film 6 — "Feedback — Specific Issues" (15 min.)

Dr. Gold discusses five specific rules "that should be sitting on the shelf of your mind ready to be brought into play on a second-by-second basis." The rules are intended to provide the trainer with some of the power needed during on-the-spot decision making. An experimental program using a driving simulator shows one of the rules in use with a learner who has severe mental retardation.

Film 7 — "Reinforcement and Influence" (15 min.)

Most trainers rely almost exclusively on some kind of reinforcement system as the primary source of power for training people. Dr. Gold argues that through artificial reinforcement trainers often further handicap their clients. He demonstrates his "no news is good news" concept and explores process influence and content influence in this most thought-provoking film.

SECTION 6

READINGS

MEALTIME

Marc and Ronna Gold

How nice, it's time to eat.
    Why do I say how nice?
Because now I won't be hungry?
Not really. Mealtime is so much more than that for me.

Mealtime is a spacer.
It's such a nice way to travel between each of the other
    moments in life.
It's a breath between getting from and going to,
And at the same time, it's somewhere to be.

It's food. The food part of a meal doesn't always have to
    be nice.
Just almost always.
I like cold things really cold.
There is only one way I really like eggs.
I like meat I can chew, but not when it chews back.
And bell peppers? Booo!

You see, I don't ask much from my food.
I just want to like it almost always.
How do you feel about food?
I've never been able to ask if you hate bell peppers, too.

If food was all there was to meals,
I don't know what I'd do.
I'd just as well eat pills.
Or I could clank my spoon.
Meals are so much more.

People are at mealtime what seasoning is on food.
Meals are for US.
US means more to me than food.
When you have as much time for me as I have for you,
Mealtime is a great time for US.
Then I don't even remember what I eat.

At other times of the day it seems that only I need you.
At those times, could I also be important for you?
Those have been times of benevolence.
Benevolence — a badly paved one-way street.
Mealtimes are not benevolent times.
Mealtimes are balanced times for US.

I hate to remember before there was US.
I'll call that WE.
That's just you and me.
Not really together — not at all US.

WE didn't balance
WE were just for the food.
I had no respect for you, and you none for me.

I wondered: Can't meals be more than food?
And dribblechin, and hurry up,
And then, and again,
You don't look at me and I won't look at you.

Then something happened — the beginning of US.
You were teaching me to use a spoon.
WE had been working on that for weeks.
I didn't know why, and you didn't either.

That day, I put a spoonful of applesauce in my ear, and
    you laughed.
You laughed so hard, I began to laugh, too.
I still don't know why you stopped laughing when you
    saw me laugh with you.

Things have been so different ever since.
I think what happened was respect.
It comes out in so many ways.

Do you know that you stopped those awful smiles you
    used to give me?
I knew they were awful because you never gave them to
    your friends.
Your voice changed, too.
It used to be squeaky, now it's you.

You didn't think I could learn anything, did you?
Since the laugh, you have come up with so many new
    things for US.
And I know you think of me more.
I think more of you, too.
That's one of the nicest things about US.
I want to learn exactly as much as you want to teach.

Did you notice that I almost cried yesterday?
I couldn't tell if you did or not.
WE are together a lot of the day.
But until yesterday, mealtime was the only time for US.

Yesterday you asked me to help you make my bed.
My God, I thought, could the bedroom be for US, too.
The way you touched me.
The way you looked at me.

I don't understand the bed yet, but I'll do anything for US.
With those awful smiles, the squeaky voice, and your
   all-day-long bits of food,
WE never got anywhere.

BUT LOOK OUT FOR US.

AN END TO THE CONCEPT OF
MENTAL RETARDATION:
OH, WHAT A BEAUTIFUL MOURNING
Marc Gold

If you could only know me for who I am
   Instead of for who I am not,
There would be so much more to see
   'Cause there's so much more that I've got.

So long as you see me as mentally retarded,
   Which supposedly means something, I guess,
There is nothing that you or I could ever do
   To make me a human success.

Someday you'll know that tests aren't built
   To let me stand next to you.
By the way you test me, all they can do
   Is make me look bad through and through.

And someday soon I'll get my chance,
   When some of you finally adapt.
You'll be delighted to know that though I'm MR,
   I'm not at all handicapped.

SECTION 7

GLOSSARY

GLOSSARY OF TERMS
RELATED TO THE TRY ANOTHER WAY SYSTEM

Artificial Reinforcement. Reinforcement not found in the natural environment, that is, under Criterion II conditions. Artificial reinforcement may be used to temporarily establish control of the learner's behavior, to accomplish Criterion I learning, or to make a transition to Criterion II. (See Motivating, p. 17.)

Assist. Trainer action in the form of verbal, gestural, or physical action to convey information to the learner about how to do the task.

Chameleon Phenomenon. The behavior a person shows at any moment reflecting who the person sees himself or herself to be at that moment. People act differently in different circumstances and are influenced by the opinions of others about them. The environments in which people who are labeled handicapped exist contribute significantly to their behavior and to their self-perceptions.

Chaining. A training format for multiple pieces of learning which involves presentation of sequential steps in a predetermined order.

    a. **Backward Chaining.** Presenting the last step or group of steps in the chain until the learner is performing them, then presenting the next-to-the-last step or group of steps in the chain, and so on, until the entire task has been learned.

    b. **Forward Chaining.** Presenting the first step or group of steps in the chain until the learner is performing them, then presenting the next step or group of steps in the chain, and so on, until the entire task has been learned.

Clustering of Steps. Starting with one or a group of steps, then adding several new steps of a task at the same time when using a chaining format. When a few steps represent a cluster, they can be taught together because the trainer believes they are best taught that way rather than as single steps. For example, when the person has learned Step 19 (the last step), then teach Steps 16, 17, and 18 together.

Competence. A skill or an attribute that someone has, that not everyone has, and that is wanted and needed by someone else.

Competence/Deviance Hypothesis. The more competence an individual has, the more deviance will be tolerated in that person by others.

Composite Learner. The presumed collection of learners for whom the Task Analysis is developed, including a description of their ages, their physical and sensory characteristics (not specific skills), and the amount of power generally required to reach criterion on tasks (for example, a small, medium, or full amount of power). (See sample Task Analyses for examples of composite learner statements.)

Content. What the learner acquires or is expected to do: either the task or the steps into which the task is divided.

Content Influence. See Trainer Intent.

Content Task Analysis. Breaking a task into teachable steps. "Teachable" refers to a judgment made by the task analyst regarding the number and size of the steps into which the task will be divided.

Correction. The information that the trainer provides to the learner following an error. The trainer may also decide to provide the information prior to the error being made if the trainer is convinced that the learner does not have the necessary information and feels that it would be more efficient.

Criterion I (CI). The predetermined point in training at which it is assumed that learning has taken place. The actual decision made by the trainer is based on characteristics of the task such as cycle length, the amount of danger involved in the task, and the differences between the environment created to teach the task (the learning environment or Criterion I environment), and the environment where the behavior will be used (the doing environment or Criterion II environment).

Criterion II (CII). Repeated demonstration or performance of the behavior under the condition(s) where it is ultimately expected to occur. The Criterion II environment is the real world.

Cycle. The total set of behaviors in a task. In a production setting, each time a worker completes one of the "products" of her job station, one work cycle has been completed.

Cycle Constancy. Reliable and consistent performance of the exact sequence of components specified for that task in the Content Task Analysis. Criterion I statements should be interpreted in terms of cycle constancy and not only in terms of ending up with the task completed correctly.

Deviance. Anything about a person that attracts negative attention or causes discomfort in other people.

Discrete Steps. Content that is distinct or absolute. What is correct can be specified and all else is incorrect. (See Nondiscrete Steps.)
   Example: Using a torque wrench, tighten the bolts to 40 foot-pounds.

Education. A process that usually takes place in a special environment so that learning can occur. An educational environment is usually different from the one where a learned task will ultimately be performed. (See Teaching and Training.)

Efficiency. Effective use of resources and time. The less time and effort it takes the trainer to let the learner know what to do, the more efficient the process. The goal is to design a process which has the most efficiency and also has sufficient power to bring the learner to criterion.

Entering Behavior. Specific skills which are critical to learning the task but which are judged by the trainer to be best taught (or known by the learner) prior to instruction on the task itself.

Expectancy. The belief on the part of a trainer as to whether or not a learner will be able to learn a task for which she has the entering behavior and for which the trainer thinks he has sufficient power and teaching time available.

Exposure. Any trainer action for informing in which a trainer expects a person to learn a task without the trainer using strategies to insure that learning occurs.
   Example: Telling a student to sharpen drill bits on a grinder until he knows how.

Fading. An instructional strategy in which the power of correction or reinforcement provided by the trainer is diminished as the performance of the learner becomes more accurate.

Feedback. Information either provided to the learner from her own actions or conveyed by the trainer to the learner after the learner's performance.

Fixture. A jig or device used as a guide or template.

Format. Organization of presentation of the content. The steps of a task may be presented to a learner one at a time, several at a time, all at once, in the order they are naturally sequenced, or in some other order. Examples of formats for single pieces of learning include match-to-sample and oddity. (See definitions.) Examples of formats for multiple pieces of learning include backward chaining, forward chaining, and total task presentation. (See definitions.) More than one format can be used for any given task.

Group Instruction. When two or more individuals with comparable entering behavior are performing and being trained simultaneously by the same trainer. In planning task analyses to be used with a group of learners, it is important to identify: (a) prerequisite skills for the task to be trained and (b) prerequisite skills for utilizing the informing strategies specified by the trainer.

Guard-band. A more narrow range of correctness than is needed for a nondiscrete step. A guard-band is specified so that after learning, performance will remain well within the real boundaries of correctness, which are wider than what has been taught as acceptable.

Example: An object must be threaded onto a shaft. Correct performance is threading from approximately ⅜ inch to approximately 1¼ inches from the end of the shaft. By training the learner to consistently thread the object between ± ½ inch and ± 1 inch from the end of the shaft, the real range of correctness is less likely to be violated.

Handedness. The predominant use of one hand.

Hierarchy of Assists. A listing of a sequence of less powerful to more powerful assists for a particular step or, in some cases, for use with all steps of a particular task. (See Informing.)

Imitation. An instructional strategy in which the learner acquires information by observing and then duplicating the behavior or performance of others, for example, the trainer. Demonstration of a task by the trainer at the beginning of training is one use of imitation. (Also called Modeling.)

Individualized (1-to-1) Instruction. Providing instruction to only one learner during a training session. Individualized instruction makes possible immediate and constant interaction between the trainer and the learner, a condition needed for maximum power.

Informing. Trainer actions intended to provide the learner with the necessary knowledge to perform the task. (See p. 15 for further discussion.)

Job Enlargement. *Vertical job enlargement* is the practice of allowing individual workers to determine their own working pace (within limits), to serve as their own inspectors by giving them responsibility for quality control, to repair their own mistakes, to be responsible for their own machine set-up and repair, and to attain choice of method. *Horizontal job enlargement* is the process of expanding the number of operations an individual worker performs at his job station.

Match-to-Sample. A format for teaching single pieces of learning which consists of presenting an object and having the learner select the one that matches from a group of objects. The choices that are used as the distractors (that is, the possible choices that are not correct) and the number of distractors used can be arranged so as to control, with precision, the level of difficulty of each match-to-sample problem.

Example: From a personal identification card taped to the wall beside a push-button phone, the learner puts one finger on the first digit of her phone number, finds one like it from among the numbers on the phone, and pushes it. The process is repeated for each of the numbers.

Mental Retardation. Mental retardation refers to a level of functioning which requires from society significantly above average training procedures and superior assets in adaptive behavior on the part of society, manifested throughout the life of both society and the individual. (See pp. 4–6 for further discussion.)

Method. The way in which a task is to be performed. (See p. 11 for further discussion.)

Modeling. See Imitation.

Motivating. Presenting objects and activities that promote desire on the part of the learner to do things. (See p. 17 for further discussion.)

Motivation. Any strategy, event, object, or activity that promotes desire on the part of the learner to do things. (See Motivating.)

Multiple Pieces of Learning. Most tasks, which consist of at least several steps or components that are connected to each other in one way or another. Most tasks require multiple pieces of learning. For example, the operation of a washing machine consists of many steps connected in a sequence. Behaving appropriately at a party consists of many steps or components which interact upon one another, but not sequentially.

Natural Reinforcement. Reinforcement that does and/or will operate in the absence of a trainer; reinforcement found under Criterion II conditions, that is, in the natural setting. (See Motivating.)

Nondiscrete Steps. Content where there is a range of correctness without definable boundaries, where a judgment is required. (See Guard-band.)
Example: Using a box wrench to tighten bolts "pretty tight."

Oddity. A format for teaching single pieces of learning in which the learner selects from a group of objects the one that does not belong. As with match-to-sample, the careful selection of the two or more distractors is important. In other words, the possible choices that are not correct allow for considerable control of the level of difficulty of the task. Varying the distractors by shape, size, color, form, category, etc., will affect the difficulty of the selection.
Example: Two large, orange, round capacitors; one small, brown, barrel-shaped resistor. Which one is different? Then one small, black, round capacitor; one small, orange, round capacitor; one small, brown, barrel-shaped resistor. Which one is different?

Organized Exposure with Feedback. A format for multiple pieces of learning which are not in a one, two, three, etc., sequence. Most social interaction skills fall into this category and can be taught through this format. Examples might include getting along at a party and eating in a restaurant. (1) When used in converting inappropriate social skills to appropriate ones, this format involves the creation of an immediate artificial environment, where Criterion I performance is obtained from the start. The learner is then sequenced through a series of environments back to the natural environment. The emphasis, in this case, is on immediately eliminating the behavior that is considered inappropriate. (2) When used in developing new social (or other) nonsequenced skills, this format involves first establishing an immediate artificial environment to simplify initial learning and then proceeding through a series of environments until Criterion II performance has been achieved. The emphasis, in this case, is on starting with a controllable environment conducive to teaching new skills of this type. In both cases the use of this format forces the trainer to clearly identify criterion performance, which is difficult to specify for such skills. Its use also requires guessing which environmental variables influence the skills. (See sample Task Analysis for Refusing Someone When He/She Tries to Borrow or Take Money, p. 47.)

Paired Associates. A format for single pieces of learning in which new components or steps are acquired by associating them with ones already known by the learner.
Example: Showing flashcards with pictures on one side and words on the other.

Power. The amount of intervention, assistance, or direction required by the trainer in order for the learner to reach criterion. (See p. 6 for further discussion.)

Prerequisite Skills. See Entering Behavior.

Private Deviance. Things that a person chooses to do privately which, if observed by others, would cause discomfort to the person doing the behavior, the people observing the behavior, or both.
Example: Picking one's nose.

Process. Everything the trainer does to teach the learner; the way in which a task is taught.

Process Task Analysis. A written description of the way the trainer will teach the content. Process Task Analysis has two subdivisions: Format and Trainer Action. (See p. 13.)

Process Influence. See Trainer Intent.

Production. Work which a person does in the absence of a trainer after learning has taken place and after Criterion I is reached. Work done for appropriate remuneration under Criterion II conditions.

Prompting.   An instructional strategy in which the trainer provides the learner with a cue or a clue as to what is correct. (See Assist.)

Propensity.   A natural inclination or tendency for the principal use of one hand.

Public Elected Deviance.   Appearance or behavior that causes discomfort to others, and that one can choose whether or not to do.
Examples: A man wearing a ponytail; using profane language in public.

Public Nonelected Deviance.   Appearance or behaviors that are not under the present control of the individual to show or not and that cause discomfort to persons observing. Much public nonelected deviance can be eliminated or reduced through training, cosmetics, or other interventions. Some public nonelected deviance is imposed on some individuals, for example, forcing adults who live in a group home to show a note for going to the doctor, or the "typical" haircut given men with Down's syndrome.
There are three subcategories of public nonelected deviance: (1) physical appearance; (2) behaviors that bring negative attention because of their presence (inappropriate behaviors); and (3) behaviors that bring negative attention because of their absence. (See Zero-Order Tasks.)
Examples: (1) Physical disability, hydrocephaly; (2) hitting oneself or others, continuous interruption of other people's conversations; (3) not eating with utensils, an adult who is unable to walk without holding someone's hand.

Recall.   A learner's giving the correct response or answer, in the absence of being provided a selection of possible choices.
Example: The learner is asked to say or write her phone number.

Recognition.   A learner is selecting the correct choice from a range of alternatives on the basis of prior training or knowledge.
Example: The learner is asked to select his phone number from three phone numbers written on a sheet of paper.

Reinforcement.   Arrangement of events that happen after a behavior (or behaviors) to increase the likelihood that the behavior (or behaviors) will be repeated under the same conditions. In the Try Another Way System, reinforcement is a subcategory of Motivation. (See p. 6 for further discussion.)

Simple Discrimination.   A format for single pieces of learning in which two or more items are presented to the learner, who then chooses the item which is correct. With this format the learner must rely exclusively on internal knowledge for making the decision, as distinguished from other formats in which some basis for comparison is presented.
Example: The learner is shown photographs of three houses and asked to point to the one in which he lives.

Simultaneous Presentation.   With formats for single pieces of learning, the concurrent presentation of visual choices.

Single Pieces of Learning.   Steps or components which can be viewed as standing alone or which the trainer feels are most efficiently taught alone.
Examples: Electronic component recognition, selection of one's house key.

Successive Presentation.   With formats for single pieces of learning, the presentation of possible choices one at a time, the learner having to decide after each item if that one is correct or not. If the choices are auditory, the presentation must be made successively, since ears cannot handle more than one choice at a time. (Try having four people each say a color to you, at exactly the same time, then name them. It is very difficult to handle simultaneous auditory information.)

Task Analysis.   All of the activity which results in there being sufficient power for the learner to acquire the task. In this manual, the capitalized term Task Analysis refers to the particular system of task analysis developed for and used in the Try Another Way System. (See p. 11 for further discussion.)

Teachable Steps.   The steps of a task that are listed in a Content Task Analysis, which reflect decisions made about the size and nature of each step of the task. When a particular step has not been learned, one option the trainer has is to subdivide the step into smaller or different steps. This means revising decisions as to what are teachable steps for the particular learner or learners involved.

Teaching.   A term used primarily in educational settings, instead of the term training. The term training is used primarily in industry or business. These terms are used interchangeably in this system. (See Training.)

Total Task Presentation.   A format for multiple pieces of learning in which the learner performs the entire task on each trial during training, and errors and assistance reduce over trials until Criterion I is reached. (This format is an alternative to the chaining formats.)

Trainer Action.   What the trainer does to teach or train a learner. It is how the learner knows what is wanted and if she is achieving it. (See p. 15 for further discussion.)

Trainer Intent.   The effects that a trainer's values, experience, mood, etc., have on his interactions with learners. Trainer intent is superimposed, consciously or unconsciously, on all trainer decisions and actions. (See p. 19 for further discussion.)

Training.   Controlled, systematic manipulations of the environment administered in such a way that the effects can be measured and which result in new skills or behaviors on the part of the learner. (See Teaching.)

Try Another Way.   A system which includes a philosophy (value system), an organizational structure for designing and carrying out training plans, and an instructional technology used to train people who find it difficult to learn. It is also a phrase used to communicate to a learner that a particular behavior was incorrect and that an alternative should be attempted. (See p. 3 for further discussion.)

Zero-Order Tasks.   Tasks or skills whose absence attracts negative attention. When zero-order tasks are maintained in their natural setting, they exist with little or no external reinforcement. Society assumes everyone will do these things; therefore, the presence of these behaviors is usually unnoticed.
    Examples: Dressing, using public transportation, bathing.

ABOUT THE AUTHOR

Marc Gold first began working with students labeled retarded as a teacher in the Los Angeles City School system. His interest led him to pursue a doctorate in experimental child psychology and special education, which he received from the University of Illinois in 1969. He then joined the faculty of the University of Illinois as a research professor working at the Institute for Child Behavior and Development. While at the Institute, Dr. Gold conducted research on the application of information from stimulus control research to the development of a vocational training technology for persons labeled moderately and severely retarded.

As an outgrowth of this research, Dr. Gold developed the "Try Another Way" system of philosophy and technology for those who find it difficult to learn. He created and now heads an organization, Marc Gold & Associates, Inc., which disseminates information about the system and trains people in its use. The system is usable with many different populations, for example, persons labeled retarded, autistic, deaf/blind, and multihandicapped, and many kinds of tasks, for example, self-help, mobility, vocational, and social tasks.